Collins

English for Business

GW00400274

RIES

Apr-2013

99

ter

SURREY
COUNTY COUNCIL

Collins

HarperCollins Publishers
77-85 Fulham Palace Road
London W6 8JB

First edition 2013

Reprint 10 9 8 7 6 5 4 3 2 1 0

© 2013 York Associates

ISBN 978–0–00–746056–4

Collins® is a registered trademark of HarperCollins
Publishers Limited

www.collinselt.com

A catalogue record for this book is available from
the British Library

Typeset in India by Aptara

Printed in China by South China Printing Co.

About the authors

Bob Dignen is a director of York Associates, a training company based in York in the north of England which offers a range of English Language, professional communication and intercultural courses, as well as seminars to develop international team and leadership skills. Bob specialises in designing and delivering seminars to develop international project team performance.

As an author, his most recent titles include *50 Ways to Improve Your Presentation Skills* and *50 Ways to Improve Your Intercultural Skills*, both published by Summertown Publishing. He is also a co-author of *English365* and *Communicating across cultures* both for Cambridge University Press, and is co-author of *Developing People Internationally*, a multimedia international training resource pack developed by York Associates.

Ian McMaster has been editor-in-chief of the bi-monthly business English magazine *Business Spotlight* since it was launched in 2001. He was also editor-in-chief of the general English magazine *Spotlight* from 1995 to 2003 and from 2006 to 2009.

He studied economics at the University of Cambridge and the London School of Economics, and is a qualified business English teacher. Since 1989, he has lived in Munich and has written widely on business and business English topics for German publications such as *Junge Karriere, Handelsblatt, Manager Seminare* and *Zeitschrift, Führung und Organization.*

His specialist research interest is the use of English as a lingua franca in business, and communication problems between native and non-native speakers.

About York Associates

The mission of York Associates is to develop people internationally. In addition to its publishing activities, it offers a wide range of training in management, communication, intercultural and language skills to private and public sector clients worldwide. It offers training and coaching to individuals and groups at its main training centre at Peasholme House, an eighteenth-century town house close to the historic centre of York in the north of England, and in-house worldwide.

About Business Spotlight

This book has been developed and published in association with *Business Spotlight*, a bi-monthly business English magazine aimed primarily at German speakers who need English in their jobs. Each issue is accompanied by an audio CD and exercise workbook (available on separate subscription). For more details and to order, see www.business-spotlight.de or write to abo@spotlight-verlag.de

About this edition

Effective International Business Communication is based on *Communicating Internationally in Business,* which was published by York Associates in association with *Business Spotlight* in 2011. Essentially this second edition focuses more specifically on the language and communication needs of non-native speakers of English.

Thanks

The authors would like to thank Will Capel for his editorial support; Steve Flinders, York Associates director, for editing the original title on which this book is based; Mike Seymour of Corporate Language Training (Cologne) for his collaboration on the online survey carried out in 2009 together with *Business Spotlight*, York Associates and Zurich Academy in Europe, which contributed to the thinking underlying the original title; and *Business Spotlight* magazine for its ongoing support for this project.

Cultural note

Both the authors were born, brought up and educated in the UK. Since then, Bob has both lived abroad and worked as an international leadership trainer with people from all over the world, although mainly from Europe; and Ian has lived and worked in Germany for more than 20 years, while travelling extensively for both business and pleasure. It is impossible for this book not to reflect their particular Eurocentric view of the world, and to show a Western orientation in its views on communication and culture. We hope that readers with different world views will engage in the debate about the issues raised in these units and accept the invitation made by Bob in his introduction to give them feedback on the content and to offer alternative views.

CONTENTS

FOREWORD

Everyone knows that English is now essential for international business. But how can non-native speakers use their English as effectively as possible in order to develop successful business relationships and, ultimately, improve the performance and the bottom line of their organisations?

That is the basic question that Bob Dignen has been seeking to answer over the past ten years, both in his training for York Associates and as a regular contributor to *Business Spotlight*, the bi-monthly magazine for German speakers who need English in their jobs.

The idea for this book grew out of a series of around 50 articles by Bob that have appeared in the Business Skills section of *Business Spotlight* over the past decade.

My collaboration with Bob on these articles – as his editor and occasional co-author – has continued the close partnership between York Associates and Spotlight Verlag publishing house that goes back to the mid 1990s. My personal thanks for this creative partnership go to everyone at York Associates, and particularly to Nick Brieger, Jeremy Comfort, Steve Flinders and, of course, Bob himself.

I am delighted that Bob's insightful articles – adapted and updated for this book – can now reach a wider audience. They make up a unique body of work looking at the business skills needed in the global workplace of the twenty-first century. They include, but go well beyond, the standard skills areas of socialising, telephoning, email, meetings, etc. And they combine advice on behavioural and language skills in a relevant and user-friendly manner.

Ian McMaster
Editor-in-chief
Business Spotlight

i.mcmaster@spotlight-verlag.de

INTRODUCTION

Who is this book for?

Effective International Business Communication has been written for non-native speakers of English with a level in English of upper-intermediate and above. The purpose of the book is simple: to help you to communicate more effectively in English at work. The book will also be helpful to business English and communication trainers of non-native speakers.

The benefits of this book

The first part of the book will enable you to get your message across more clearly when speaking. It will also help you to listen in ways that will create better understanding with colleagues and business partners. We look at how to communicate with native speakers, and also with people whom you may regard as 'difficult'.

In the second part of the book, we give you ideas on how to improve core business communication skills – building relationships, networking, influencing, making decisions, managing conflict and building trust.

The third part looks at different aspects of virtual communication, including advice on how to write better emails and how to manage conference calls.

The aim of the book is not to make you a perfect English speaker. Many native English speakers are not very good at communicating internationally despite the fact that they speak the language (more or less) correctly. Their English is often less effective than that of non-native English speakers: it can be over-complex, spoken too quickly, and full of confusing vocabulary and abbreviations. Your goal should be to use the English you know to communicate clearly and respectfully to others.

Communication is situational

All communication is situational, which means that there are no do's and don'ts in international communication: you need to adapt your message and the way you communicate to each specific situation. The book does give you guidelines and strategies for effective communication with examples of language for you to consider (in the *What do you say?* sections at the end of most units). But it is up to you to decide what to say and how to say it, according to your assessment of the specific context. Each situation has three main elements:

1 Culture

Think about the values, behaviours and communication styles that you are likely to meet in each different situation. Try to understand the different attitudes to time, to organisation, to teamwork, to decision-making, to relationships and to hierarchy, which shape how people communicate. It is not only national cultural differences which can have an impact on your chances of successful communication. Organisational culture, professional culture and other layers of culture can also be significant. When you have analysed the cultural context in which you are working, then you can decide how much you need to adapt your own communication style to that context.

2 Person

Consider the unique individual(s) in front of you. Cultural knowledge gives you only very general information about attitudes and behaviours. Try to understand the specific personalities of the people you work with and to adapt your communication style and strategy to these individuals as well.

3 Business context

Professional people work to get results. The business context may lead us to cooperate with some people, but may put us into conflict with others, so skills like influencing and managing conflict are also essential when we work internationally. We always have to think about the business environment when we choose our communication strategy, and we have to balance our interests against those of others. At York Associates, we call this 'achieving results through relationships'.

This book is primarily written for people communicating in English for business internationally. However, I have been told that my training is not international but *inter-human*. In other words, you will also be able to apply many of the ideas and approaches in this book in your own language, and in private as well as in business contexts. After all, communication doesn't stop when we leave the office.

Feedback

Good communicators always ask for feedback. So please let us know your thoughts, whether positive or negative, after reading this book. We want to learn from you too, so we look forward to hearing from you.

Bob Dignen
Director
York Associates

bob.dignen@york-associates.co.uk

1 SPEAKING

> **It is impossible to speak in such a way that you cannot be misunderstood.**
>
> Karl Popper, Austro-British philosopher (1902–94)

Successful communication is a challenge for us all. When we speak, we have to think a lot about how to get our message across clearly to others.

In this unit we look at some of the principles of clear speaking and at some strategies that will help you to communicate more successfully internationally. You will have the opportunity to profile your speaking style and identify the factors that may make it difficult for people to understand you. You will also be able to develop a personal development plan to become a better speaker.

Before you read on, think about these questions:

1 How can I make sure that other people understand what I want to say?

2 What kind of communication style do I have? For example, do I speaking fast or slow and do I use long or short sentences?

3 Is there anything in the way that I speak that makes it difficult for other people to understand me?

Understanding the speaking challenge

The quotation from Karl Popper highlights the fact that there is always a communication gap between what speakers say and what listeners understand. This is caused by the process of interpretation, as we can see in the classic sender-receiver model of communication:

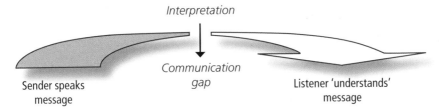

Interpretation

Communication
gap

Sender speaks
message

Listener 'understands'
message

Senders of messages (speakers) need to recognise that whatever they say will be interpreted by receivers (listeners) and can be misunderstood. Misunderstanding may be due to language reasons: a word can be wrongly translated, or perhaps the pronunciation is unclear. But cultural differences, personality factors and aspects of the environment (for example, a poor telephone connection) can also lead to misinterpretation.

As speakers, we need to be sensitive to the different perspectives of listeners. We need to know what they value, what their interests are, what information they can understand, and which forms of communication they see as polite and clear.

TIPS for successful speaking

To be successful, speakers need to communicate the right things in a clear and sensitive way to listeners. So as speakers, we should think carefully about both our own needs *and* the needs of listeners when building and delivering our messages. If we do this, there is a better chance that listeners will:

- understand us
- act on what we say
- be more motivated and more convinced by what we have to say
- feel more trusting toward us.

To be successful, speakers should focus on four main dimensions in their communication, which we can call **TIPS**:

- **T**arget
- **I**nformation
- **P**rocess
- **S**tyle

1 Target

Problems often occur in international business because people misunderstand the objective behind a message. These misunderstandings can happen even with simple questions such as *Have you finished that report yet?* Is this simply a question to check the status of the report, or is there an underlying push, even a criticism, because the report is overdue?

There is a story of how an employee in Germany completely misinterpreted the meaning of one sentence spoken by his American CEO during a webcast. The CEO finished with this invitation:

If you have any comments on this webcast or about the organisation, please contact me.

The CEO's intention was not to make an invitation to people to give very detailed feedback on the webcast, but more to provide a polite and formulaic ending. But the German employee interpreted this as a serious invitation. He responded by writing a long email detailing what he saw as serious problems in the organisation, including poor communication from the management in his local area. The result was a strong reprimand from his immediate boss, who had received a less than friendly call from the head office in the US.

Good practice 1   State your objective clearly.

Here are five key tips to help you to make sure that your international colleagues understand what your objectives are when you talk to them.

1 Give enough background information so that the listener can interpret your message correctly.
2 State your main message in a way that the other sees as polite.
3 Use positive language.
4 Make it clear what you are *not* talking about in order to avoid misinterpretation.
5 Show that you recognise and appreciate the listener's situation.

Be clear, be sensitive

Even when the objective is clear to the speaker, communication can fail if the speaker does not think about the listener's view. Speakers often focus too much on their own agendas.

A good example is the way many managers communicate about change. They often communicate the official messages about cost savings but do not talk enough about the fears of those experiencing the change. They should spend more time explaining the impact of the savings on everyday working life and talking through the practical steps that people could take to deal with the changes.

This focus on the listener is one of the keys to successful speaking. Treat listeners as your 'communication customers' and try to find a way to take their needs and expectations into account in your messages.

Good practice 2   Adapt the way you express your objective to the listener.

Balance your needs as a speaker against those of the listener.

2 Information

Once speakers are clear about their objectives, the next step is to think carefully about the information they want to communicate. Listeners may view information in very different ways, according to their cultural background and what they already know. The two key dimensions are what information to communicate, and how extensive and complex this information should be.

Which information?

Successful speakers say things that are relevant to their listeners. If what is said is not relevant, listeners quickly switch off because they cannot see the point of listening.

Good practice 3   Select information that is interesting and useful for the listener.

Successful speakers talk about things in a way which makes the job of listening easy.

How much information and how complex?

Successful speakers communicate things that are understandable. Otherwise, listeners are likely to become confused and demotivated, and stop listening. This will certainly happen if you give too much information or if your information is too complex. So speakers need to adapt what they say to the preferences, knowledge and competence of their listeners.

Good practice 4   K.I.S.S.S.S.

One golden rule of good communication is K.I.S.S. (Keep It Short and Simple), but good communicators go further: they use K.I.S.S.S.S. This means: Keep It ...
- Short,
- Simple,
- Structured, and
- Several times repeated.

Good practice 5   Communicate the right information and the right amount of information.

Not all information is useful information. Bear in mind the language ability and the professional needs and preferences of different listeners when you choose how much information to give and how complex this information should be.

3   Process

Communication is a process of interaction between speakers and listeners. This process includes the rules and procedures that people follow in different situations. For example, in one department or organisation, meeting processes might involve starting on time and inviting everyone to summarise their activities since the last meeting. In another department or organisation, meetings might involve waiting for the boss to arrive and then listening to him or her talk at length before anyone else speaks. When people from one meetings culture work with those from another, they need to agree on a new process that suits them both.

Communicating successfully internationally means defining and managing processes in meetings, telephone calls, presentations, negotiations, one-to-one social conversations, and so on. All these situations have three basic phases: an opening, a middle and an end. For language suggestions for these and other situations, see the *What do you say?* section at the end of this unit.

Good practice 6   Manage the process as well as the content of communication.

Successful speakers use standard expressions to manage the process of typical business communication situations.

Let us look more closely at the process involved in presentations, which can vary greatly between cultures, whether national or organisational. Some audiences sit in respectful silence until the speaker has finished; other audiences want to get involved and comment, add their own experiences, and ask lots of questions. And members of other audiences may feel that it is perfectly acceptable to talk to each other while the speaker is talking.

As the speaker, you need to be sensitive to these different expectations. If you are not, you may manage the process in a way that frustrates, irritates or confuses the audience. Good international speakers explicitly negotiate the communication process so that everyone is clear about what is going to happen. They do this by:

1 Negotiating the question process in a presentation: *Would you prefer to ask questions during the presentation, or shall we leave questions to the end?*
2 Clarifying the place of decision-making in a meeting: *Just to clarify, are we planning to take a decision today, or is this just a preliminary meeting?*
3 Clarifying what is polite to ask in social situations: *Can I ask you about your family? I hope I'm not being rude by asking this, am I?*

According to the INCA (Intercultural Competence Assessment) project, this form of explicit rule management is a key intercultural competence. INCA states that a fully interculturally competent individual 'is able to relate problems of intercultural action to conflicting communication conventions; is able to identify and is ready to adapt to new discourse rules to prevent or clarify misunderstandings'.

> **Good practice 7   When there are different expectations, negotiate an agreed process of communication.**
>
> The negotiation of a process may sometimes seem time-consuming or even unnecessary. But conflicting expectations can lead to significant misunderstanding, so in the long run it is worth spending extra time negotiating the process.

Turn-taking principles

In their book *Riding the Waves of Culture: Understanding Cultural Diversity in Business*, Fons Trompenaars and Charles Hampden Turner describe models of turn taking in meetings in different national cultures. The graphic below describes three simplified patterns found in different business cultures:

Different patterns of turn taking during meetings

The first pattern characterises a way of speaking often found in Germany: long, strong, and rich in detail. When one person speaks, others listen silently, before someone else starts on another long turn.

The second pattern is said to be more common in Sweden: less dominated by single speakers, shorter and sharper than the German pattern, but with listeners similarly silent. The longer silences between the turns may signal greater respect and caution in a more collectivist culture, and an unwillingness to stand out as a stronger individual than the rest.

The final pattern is said to be more common in France: longer, more expansive and more adversarial. In this pattern, speakers explore ideas and options from different perspectives and are more tolerant of interruptions from listeners.

Misunderstandings can clearly occur when these different types of communicator meet. Type 3s may find type 1s rather machine-like and uncreative. Type 1s and type 2s may see type 3s as rather disorganised, and rude in the way they interrupt and talk over others. Type 2s may be seen by both type 1s and type 3s as distant and difficult to engage.

Of course, these clashes may not (only) be the result of intercultural differences. They can also happen as a result of differences in personal communication style, for example, between a very talkative and unstructured extrovert on the one hand, and a very careful, concise and structured introvert on the other.

An international model: the interactive dialogue model

For dialogue to work effectively, there needs to be cooperation between the speaker and the listener. Take a look at the interactive dialogue model below, where the communication process is managed carefully to build mutual understanding.

The interactive dialogue model

Person 1 and Person 2 have a conversation. Person 1 starts talking and Person 2 listens. As a speaker, Person 1 **does not talk for too long**, and finishes talking with an active handover to Person 2 using a question, e.g. *'What do you think?'*. The aim is to check understanding and involve the listener, creating interactive dialogue.

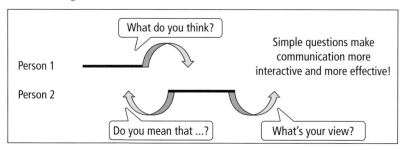

Person 2 **does not disagree** or give an opinion immediately and **takes time to clarify** or reformulate what has been said, by asking Person 1 a question, e.g. *'Do you mean that … ?'*. This checks understanding and shows respect for Person 1's ideas. Then Person 2 can give an opinion. They avoid talking for too long and hand back actively after speaking with a short question, e.g. *'What's your view?'*. And so the process continues.

Note

In this model both Person 1 and Person 2 **listen actively**, using phrases to show understanding (*'I see'*) and interest (*'That's important because …'*). This builds a clearer and more positive dialogue.

4 Style

The final dimension that speakers have to consider is to what extent their personal speaking style is effective in their international contacts. People speak in different ways for both psychological reasons (for example, because they are more extrovert or more introvert) and because of cultural influences (for example, they have learned to be direct because their corporate culture is highly task-oriented).

Use the analysis below to profile yourself and reflect on your own communication style. It can encourage you to get feedback and to think more strategically about how you communicate internationally.

Your speaking style

Think about the way you speak in professional situations and work through these five steps. You will, of course, speak differently from one work situation to another, so try to think about how you speak *typically*.

1 Circle the word in each pair below that best describes your speaking style:

Physical	Fast	Slow
	Loud	Quiet
	Energetic	Calm
	Touching	Distant
	Smiling	Serious
Informational	Long and complex	Short and simple
	Analytical	Results-oriented
	Structured	Flexible
	Direct	Indirect
	Time-focused	Time-flexible
Psychological	Introvert	Extrovert
	Impersonal	Personal
	Open	Closed
	Emotional	Neutral
	Pushing	Helping

2 Ask an international colleague if he or she agrees with your self-evaluation.

3 Now that you have a picture of your style, note down how different international partners might interpret it (the positives and the negatives).

4 Think about how you may need to adapt your personal speaking style for your next meeting, presentation or negotiation in line with the results of point 3.

5 After your next meeting, negotiation, presentation, etc., get feedback from someone on your communication style. Were you clear? Did you have a positive or a negative impact? Then decide on an area that you need to improve.

It's not what you say, it's the way that you say it

The tone of your voice, your speech rhythm and your volume can significantly change the way in which people understand and interpret your words. Look at the ways in which these voice characteristics may be interpreted:

Volume Some people think that loud speakers are arrogant.
Tone Some people think that a hard tone is aggressive.
Pitch Some people think that a lower pitch signals strength or maturity.
Fillers Some people think that sounds like 'uh' or little laughs show insecurity.

Ask yourself:

- What impact does your voice have on your business partners?
- What impressions and assumptions might it generate?
- Which of the above dimensions would be it useful for you to adapt?

The final word

Successful speakers have a wide range of skills. These skills need to be complemented by effective listening skills and by non-verbal communication skills in terms of appropriate body language, facial expressions and gestures. Listening is the subject of the next unit.

Successful speaking for non-native English speakers also requires the right attitude:

- Balance speaking with writing. Avoid email if it is better to talk to people. Use email communication (see Units 11 and 12) to follow up discussions by phone and in meetings.
- Have the courage to speak in the first place. Non-native speakers often fear that they will make mistakes or do not want to struggle to say complex things with too few words. As a result, native speakers may dominate international meetings and conference calls (see Unit 4).

As a non-native speaker, there is no need for you to speak like a native speaker. Your objective instead is to become a clear international speaker. Indeed, many native speakers of English are not clear international speakers. If you have an intermediate level of English, and combine it with the skills discussed in this unit, you can make *your* communication clearer to other non-native speakers than that of many native speakers!

What do you say?

State your objective clearly

Sample telephone call:

> *I've just had a call from Akash in India about a seminar they'd like to organise for IT staff involved in the SAP project. He'd like you to run a workshop in July.*
>
> *He wants you to run it because he knows you've done it before, and he's had good feedback from previous seminars. I don't want to put you under pressure with this. I know you're very busy at the moment. What do you think? Is it possible?*

Give enough background information for the listener to be able to interpret the message correctly
- *I've just had a call from Akash in India about a seminar they'd like to organise for IT staff involved in the SAP project.*

State the main message in a way which the other sees as polite
- *He'd like you to run a workshop in July.*

Motivate
- *He wants you to run it because he knows you've done it before, and he's had good feedback from previous seminars.*

Say what you are not saying in order to avoid misinterpretation
- *I don't want to put you under pressure with this.*

Include appreciation of the circumstances of the listener.
- *I know you're very busy at the moment.*

Negotiate and ask for feedback
This sends a clear message that you are *not* simply telling someone what to do:
- *What do you think? Is it possible?*

Adapt the way you express your objective to the listener

Should I inform ...	... or do I need to sell?
Just to let you know ...	*I think this is useful because ...*
Do I have to implement ...	**... or is it better to negotiate?**
We have to ...	*Do you think we can ...*
Should I focus on the task ...	**... or wait and build the relationship?**
Let's get down to business.	*Another coffee?*
Is it better to speak ...	**... or is it time to listen?**
In my opinion ...	*What's your opinion?*

K.I.S.S.S.S.

We make it easier for people to listen to us if we keep our messages short, simple, structured and the same – by "the same', we mean repeat key words or parts of the message. Here is an example of what we mean:

There are two main problems: firstly, a lack of budget, and secondly, a lack of resources. And with both problems, budget and resources, I don't think we can meet the current project deadline.

Manage the process as well as the content of communication

	Email	Telephone call	Meeting	Presentation	Social conversation
Opening Start	*Dear Fiona*	*Good morning. Could I speak to Jeremy?*	*OK, everyone. To begin, …*	*I think I should make a start.*	*Hi, can I say hello? I'm …*
Polite comment	*Hi everyone, I hope all is well with you.*	*Hi Jeremy. How are you? How's the weather in England?*	*I'd like to welcome Johan and Andrea. They are with us to …*	*Nice to see everyone here today.*	*Nice to meet you.*
Objective	*I am just writing to …*	*I'm just calling to …*	*As you can see from the agenda, the objective of today's meeting is to …*	*What I want to do today is …*	*So tell me a little bit about yourself. Are you here on business?*
Timing	*I know you're busy but …*	*We'll just need a few minutes …*	*In terms of timing, we have scheduled …*	*I plan to talk for around …*	*Are you busy?*
Interaction	*I'd really appreciate your help …*	*Are you free at the moment?*	*In terms of procedure, Johan will chair the first part and then hand over to …*	*If you have any questions, …*	*What about you? Are you …?*

	Email	Telephone call	Meeting	Presentation	Social conversation
Middle Input	We have a problem with a key customer ...	There are just a couple of things ...	The first thing I would like to discuss is ...	The first point I want to talk about is ...	Did you see the news last night about ...?
Clarification	If that's not clear, do come back to me.	Did you say ...?	Can I clarify one thing?	Does anyone have any questions at this point?	Sorry, I don't understand. What do you mean?
Conclusion	If you could get back to me before the end of the week, it would be great.	OK. I'll call you back later today.	OK, so can we all agree to ...	So, in conclusion, I would like to repeat that ...	That's great. Dinner at eight next week then.
Close relationship	I look forward to hearing from you.	Talk to you tomorrow then.	Thank you all for your contributions.	If you have any further questions, don't hesitate to contact me by email.	It was nice seeing you.
Formal end	Best regards,	Bye.	See you at the next meeting.	Thank you for listening.	Bye.

The interactive dialogue model

The speaker hands over with simple phrases to keep the dialogue moving
- *What do you think?*
- *Do you see what I mean?*
- *How do you see it?*

The listener shows understanding and interest (verbally)
- *I see.*
- *That's interesting.*
- *I agree.*

The listener shows understanding and interest (non-verbally) with
- *eye contact*
- *facial expression*
- *nodding ...*

The listener clarifies what the speaker has said with simple questions
- *What do you mean ...?*
- *Why do you say that ...?*

2 LISTENING

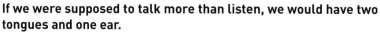

If we were supposed to talk more than listen, we would have two tongues and one ear.

Mark Twain, American author and humorist (1835–1910)

Listening is the foundation of effective communication. As children, we learn to listen before we can speak, read or write. But many professional people have rather poor listening skills. They sometimes find it difficult to concentrate on what the other person is saying. Perhaps they have little real interest in the other person's ideas. Often they are impatient to start talking themselves and give their own point of view. Whatever the reason, this lack of listening leads to misunderstanding, conflict and inefficiency in the workplace.

In this unit we look at the nature and purpose of listening, and at how to become a more effective listener. Before you read on, think about these questions:

Q
1 Why should we listen to other people?
2 What kind of listener are you?
3 What stops us from listening effectively?
4 How can you become a better listener?

Reasons for listening

Let us look at the benefits of listening effectively:

1 To get the information we need to complete a task

This is the most obvious reason for listening at work, and people generally do this quite well. It typically means listening silently, with occasional questions to check the accuracy of the information given, before going away to do a job. This is a kind of listening that generally benefits the listener more than the speaker, which is probably why it is easier to do.

2 To assess competence and trustworthiness

This is a key reason for listening in the business world. It involves analysing the expertise and the attitudes of speakers, and making judgements about them.

3 To show competence and trust

As listeners, we want to demonstrate our own expertise by showing that we understand complex issues. We also want to show our approach to business through positive agreement or constructive disagreement with what the speaker says.

4 To show respect and to build rapport

Taking time to listen to others is an act of respect, and shows your commitment to your relationship with the other person. However, listening styles differ. For example, speakers from more task-oriented cultures may expect listeners to show respect by being silent. On the other hand, people from more relationship-oriented cultures may expect listeners to be more active and to show a positive attitude, for example, by making comments like *That's interesting*. Using the wrong listening style can lead to confusion. Silent listening may be misinterpreted by a relationship-oriented speaker as a sign of hostility. Verbal feedback may be perceived as unnecessary 'noise' by a task-oriented listener.

5 To monitor the speaker's style in order to achieve better communication

The focus here is less on content than style. The objective is to analyse the speaker's verbal and non-verbal behaviour. Which words do they use? How fast do they speak? Is their message structured? How aware is the speaker of the listener? What kind of body language do they use? Listeners can then adapt their own styles to the speaker's, so that the speaker feels more comfortable and open communication is easier.

6 To understand how to influence others

Effective motivators and influencers try to understand other people's interests before speaking. For example, good salespeople often start by asking questions and listening carefully to the answers before trying to sell.

7 To empathise

Speakers sometimes just want a listener 'to be there for them', that is, to listen to the problem, to show understanding, and to share a difficult experience. In this role, the listener is primarily supportive of the other person, without having any personal advantage or interest.

8 To understand the mindset of the other person

This is about listening 'between the lines', that is, listening to what is *not* said, and analysing the attitudes, assumptions and values of the speaker. What do their words tell us about their attitudes to leadership, to teamwork, to business relationships, to risk, or to time? These things may not be said, but someone with a sensitive ear can learn a lot about them by listening.

9 To hear if our ideas are understood and valued

As listeners, we can also evaluate our own performance as speakers. When others misunderstand what we are saying, we need to deliver our ideas in another way. Of course, it may be that our ideas have indeed been understood but not accepted. So we also need to listen carefully for any clash of assumptions or values.

10 To give pleasure

Do people generally enjoy talking to you? Do others say that you are an easy person to talk to? Do people walk away from meetings with you with smiles on their faces? If people are motivated to talk to you, you are more likely to get the best from them. This means we need to reflect. Are we listening in a way which is motivating for the other person?

The ROI (Return On Investment) on listening effectively in the workplace	
Better relationships with more trust	Improved quality
More motivated staff	More efficient information flow
Higher productivity	Fewer mistakes and lower costs
Increased creativity	Happier customers

What kind of listener are you?

It is essential to be aware of your own listening style and of the impact that your style may have on others. Read these descriptions of three different kinds of listener below and decide which style is closest to yours.

People-focused listeners

This kind of listener focuses on supporting the speaker by being attentive to feelings and needs. He or she has a lot of patience and asks questions such as

What do you think? or *How do you feel about this?* This helps speakers to give their views and to feel that they are being listened to. This person-oriented style may, however, seem unfocused to information-oriented and results-oriented speakers, who may not like too many 'vague' questions about feelings.

Information-oriented listeners

This kind of listener likes to collect and analyse information in order to understand the situation as fully as possible. They usually take the time to listen to all the information so that the right decision can be taken. This analytical approach may, however, overlook the emotional attitudes behind the information and seem cold or unsympathetic to some speakers.

Results-oriented listeners

The main interest for these listeners is to achieve their goals as quickly and efficiently as possible. They often have little patience for what they see as irrelevant information, and can be frustrated by speakers who talk for too long in an 'unfocused' way. Some speakers, especially those who expect listeners to show empathy or analytical skills, may see results-oriented listeners as pushy and arrogant.

Which type of listener are you primarily?

What stops us from listening effectively

Read the Speaker-Listener dialogues below and think about why listening is not happening effectively in each case. Think in terms of the message, the speaker and the listener. Then refer to the answer key for our analysis.

Dialogue 1
Speaker: *So, what do you think about my recommendation on pricing?*
Listener: *What? Oh, sorry. Look, I'm not sure I'm the right person to ask.*
Speaker: *But you're in charge of sales, aren't you?*
Listener: *Yes, but I'm really busy now. Can we discuss this tomorrow?*

Dialogue 2
Speaker: *So, the fifth aspect of this problem is ...*
Listener: *Sorry to interrupt, but what was the fourth aspect? I didn't catch that.*
Speaker: *The fourth aspect was finance. Remember?*
Listener: *Oh, that was number four. Sorry. Are there many more points?*

Dialogue 3
Speaker: *I think we need to look at the terrible problem that we have in our team.*
Listener: *I don't think we should use the word 'problem' here.*
Speaker: *OK, well let's say 'issue' then. We need to discuss how we can ...*
Listener: *Sorry, but this is a decision for the team leader, not for us. I suggest we arrange a meeting with her as soon as possible.*

Becoming a better listener

The key to becoming a better listener is *attitude*. We need to believe that other people are really worth listening to, and that it is important to give others the chance to express themselves. We need to believe that it is useful to engage with others, and that both speaker and listener can learn and benefit from dialogue. Otherwise there is little chance of developing good listening skills.

Let us look at 11 principles of effective listening:

1 Empty your mind of your own thoughts when the other person begins to speak

Make yourself concentrate fully on what is being said. Focus on hearing interesting and important information. Try to discover the different levels of meaning in the message: move from the information on the surface to considering the feelings, attitudes and needs of the speaker. Respect what is said and see this as an opportunity to learn something new about the person.

2 Support the start of a conversation by encouraging others to talk

Do this by asking questions, as this creates golden opportunities for listening. You can tailor the kind of question you ask to your listening objective. For example, do you want to get information, assess the competence or mentality of the speaker, or build rapport?

3 Give others time to say what they want to say

Remember that it often takes longer to get ideas across in a foreign language: words have to be remembered, and sentences have to be formed. Try to become comfortable with the silence that others may need in order to formulate their ideas.

4 Respond to what is said

When we listen, we need to make two basic types of response. We need to show that we understand what has been said (*I understand*); and that we value what has been said (*I think this is important because ...*). Otherwise, speakers may become confused or unwilling to go on talking to us.

5 Give positive feedback, both verbal and non-verbal, in ways that the speaker will interpret as positive

Opinions about what makes positive feedback vary according to cultural norms and personality preferences. For example, what does silence mean? Does it indicate interested concentration or a lack of interest, or even hostility? Comments such as *Yes, that's interesting* or *Really?* may be intended and seen as a sign of positive politeness in some contexts, but as superficial and not genuine in others. Non-verbal behaviours, such as strong eye contact or smiling at the speaker, may also be viewed positively or negatively, depending on cultural context and personal preferences. Monitor the impact of your listening style and adapt it if it seems to be confusing or negative.

6 Clarify what is said

Never assume that you have understood something correctly. It is particularly important to clarify when working in a foreign language because speakers often do not use the words they really need. Also, when working internationally, it is sometimes difficult to understand the motivation of business partners, who may have very different values, attitudes and interests.

7 Use the 'keyword approach' to listening

Listen carefully to the words the speaker uses, and then use some of the same words to develop the conversation. This technique is not just about clarifying. If speakers hear their own words reflected back in a question or a comment, this can increase comfort and trust.

The following dialogue illustrates this technique. The words in bold are the key words that Natasha picks up from Karl's comments and uses to guide the conversation. This form of listening is a simple but powerful technique for keeping the listener concentrated and the speaker energised.

Karl: OK, I'd like to focus on pricing in this meeting. We may need to reduce our prices a little next year.

Natasha: When you say 'a little', Karl, how much do you mean? One or two of our main competitors radically undercut us in some markets.

Karl: You're right. I was thinking mainly of the French and the German markets, which are so important for us.

Natasha: OK, so shall we focus on the French and German markets for the moment? What do you suggest?

Karl: My feeling is that we need to look at a price cut of around ten per cent if we want to attract new customers who view us as too expensive at the moment.

Natasha: That's interesting. Of course, if we're talking about attracting new customers, maybe we need to think about a different strategic approach.

8 Develop conversations by asking questions and making relevant comments

Good listeners create opportunities for listening. Make sure that you engage others by asking questions that invite them to talk in depth about topics that they find interesting, not simply to deliver information that is interesting to you. Be careful, however, not to turn conversations into interviews by asking too many questions and putting pressure on the speaker.

9 Give yourself feedback on your own listening performance

Ask yourself the following questions as you listen. Am I fully concentrating on the other person or am I letting my mind wander away? Am I becoming impatient?

Am I disagreeing too quickly with what is being said? Am I spending too much time preparing counter-arguments in my head? Am I asking the right questions and paying enough attention to the feelings behind the words? Self-coaching when listening is a good way to keep yourself engaged.

10 Know when to stop listening and end the conversation

Summarise as much as necessary to avoid any misunderstandings. Make sure that the conversation ends positively.

11 Control yourself

Keep your negative emotions under control, even if you feel the speaker is attacking you or not showing you respect. Try to remain calm and engaged by asking questions. Recognise that it may not be the speaker's intention to cause these feelings. Stop yourself saying *Yes, but …* – this could be a sign that you have stopped listening.

Try not to interrupt or otherwise disturb the speaker or communicate disrespect. Listen to yourself listening, and if you hear any of the unconstructive thoughts below, switch them off and re-engage with the speaker.

Rejection of relevance:	*This is boring.*
Contradiction:	*Yes, but …*
Changing the subject:	*That's enough about this. Let's talk about …*
Denial of feelings:	*You don't need to worry about that.*
Transfer to self:	*Let me tell you about something that happened to me.*
Advising:	*All you have to do is …*
Focus on time:	*I have other things to do.*

Energise yourself physically. If you feel tired or start to lose interest, move, change position, stand up and walk around if you can, breathe deeply a few times, or alter the mood of the moment by asking a provocative or fun question.

Take notes to maintain your concentration when listening to a long presentation or to a lot of speakers during a meeting. Structuring a speaker's ideas with some form of visual representation (bullet points, boxes, mind maps) is also a good way to improve your understanding and to remain engaged.

Are you ready to start listening?

Effective listening needs commitment, effort and skill. The fact that so many professional people listen badly creates big risks – for leaders, teams, projects and profitability. So how long does it take someone to become a better listener? Well, a karate instructor once said that he had to practise a new move 10,000 times before he had truly perfected it and it became an internalised competence that he could perform automatically. The message is clear. Becoming a good listener is a long journey for most of us. So why not make your next conversation your first step on your road to becoming a great listener?

What do you say?

Good reasons for listening

Effective listeners create opportunities for listening by encouraging others with questions at the beginning of a conversation.

Getting the information we need
- *Who is responsible for ...?*
- *Who looks after this?*
- *How much will it cost to ...?*
- *When will you finish ...?*
- *How long will you need to ...?*

Assessing competence
- *How long have you been working in this area?*
- *What's your background?*
- *Have you ever ...?*

Building rapport
- *So when did you arrive?*
- *Is this your first time in ...?*
- *Can I get you something to drink before we start?*
- *I agree with you about that.*
- *Yes, I also think that we should ...*

Empathising
- *I see.*
- *I understand.*
- *I understand what you're saying. And in my experience, ...*
- *It's interesting what you say about ...*
- *What you just said is very important because ...*
- *That must be difficult / interesting / tough / ...*
- *How did / do you feel about this?*

Understanding mindsets
- *What do you think of ...?*
- *What's your opinion about ...?*
- *Do you feel that ...?*

Becoming a better listener

Supporting the start of a conversation
- *Do you have a lot of experience in ...?*
- *What do you think of ...?*
- *Is this your first time in ...?*

Non-verbal listening

Think about the non-verbal features of listening below and how differences in culture and personality can affect they way they are used in listening:

- Smiling
- Eye contact
- Facial expression
- Posture
- Gestures
- Head movements
- Silence
- How close people stand / sit

Clarifying information

- *Do you mean that ...?*
- *So, if I've understood you correctly, your company has ...?*
- *Could you clarify exactly when / what / how / who / why ...?*
- *Are you saying that ...?*

Clarifying motivation

- *So what is most important for you here is to ...*
- *Does this mean that ideally you would like to ...?*
- *Your main interest in this software project is to ...? Is that right?*

The 'keyword approach'

Listen for the keywords that people use in their messages and then use these words as a starting point for clarification:

- *You said before that you needed the information urgently. What exactly do you mean by 'urgently'?*
- *You said you felt a little disappointed by the results of the survey. Why do you say 'disappointed'?*
- *You said that it's important to be honest in discussions. Can you tell me what you mean by 'honesty' here?*

Using questions and comments to develop a conversation

Effective listeners develop conversations by:

Listening to motivate

- *Tell me a little bit more about ...*
- *So, you really like Spain. Are you planning to go again soon?*

Listening to influence

- *I think you need to ...*
- *In my experience, it's important to ...*

Listening as a coach
- *What would be your ideal solution to this?*
- *What have you tried so far to solve this problem?*
- *What else do you think you could do to improve things?*
- *Is there another way of solving this?*

Summarising and closing

Formal and informal conversations end in different ways. Effective listeners know how and when to end a discussion.

Initiating the end
- *Right, … (pause)*
- *Good, well, … (pause)*
- *OK, well, I think I should be going.*

Summarising
- *So to summarise, this means that …*
- *So, just to check, we'll …*
- *Shall we just summarise where we've got to? I'll …*

Closing positively
- *Nice talking to you.*
- *See you later.*
- *Good luck with the project.*

3 BUILDING RELATIONSHIPS

If you can be interested in people, you can own the world.

Jay Abraham, US marketing expert

Relationship-building skills can be as important for professional success as technical skills. It is vital for us to think carefully about how we build and develop positive, lasting relationships with the people whom we work with – colleagues, managers, suppliers, customers and others.

In this unit we focus on how to manage the first face-to-face meeting with a new contact, the opening moments of a business relationship. In following units in this section we look at other dimensions to professional relationships including networking and building trust.

Before you read on, think about these questions:

1 How do you build professional relationships? What is your style?

2 What are the phases of developing a conversation with a new business contact?

3 Are there any differences in the way that men and women build professional relationships?

4 What specific skills do you need to build relationships across cultures?

Relationship-building styles

People at work have very different views of what professional relationships are for. As a result, they approach first meetings with very different ideas about the kind of relationship they want to develop. Some want to become friends quickly. Others view their private lives as completely separate from the office and work relationships. These different preferences are influenced by both personality and cultural factors.

On the one hand, people who are very focused on results may well place less emphasis on relationships. On the other hand, people who place a lot of emphasis on relationships may need to remind themselves, or to be reminded, of the main reason for working – to get results.

People from more collectivist cultures may emphasise group ties more than those from more individualist cultures. Different attitudes to hierarchy will also have an impact. Senior people in more authoritarian cultures may expect formal deference to be shown to them in first meetings, while more senior people in more egalitarian cultures may well prefer a much more informal approach.

The four primary motivations for relationship building

Elias Porter, creator of relationship awareness theory, is an expert in the psychology of interpersonal relationships. He says that people are driven by very different motivations to form and develop relationships. Understanding these different motivations can help us to manage first meetings more effectively.

Try to identify your own main relationship motivation and communication style from the four descriptions below. While you are reading, think about what other people may like or dislike about your relationship-building style.

Motivation type 1: Supportive-Caring

For these people, the main motivation in building relationships is to support and help others. They feel good when they see others feeling good. In first meetings with visitors to the office, for example, they may make a lot of effort to check that other people are happy. They offer coffee, check if accommodation arrangements are fine, are keen to offer extra help, and so on. They may ask a lot of polite questions to make others feel welcome and accepted. They like to talk about what other people want to talk about.

Warning!

These people may appear to some others as superficial and too friendly, perhaps even as nervous or lacking in confidence. But remember that their aim is to make others happy.

Motivation type 2: Assertive-Directing

For these people, the main motivation in building relationships is to get things done, to get results by influencing other people, to organise, and to make an impact. They see themselves as capable and in charge, ambitious and persuasive. In first meetings they are happy to talk and be heard. They can be very motivated when there is an exchange of opinions on a topic that they feel they know something about. They are happy to listen to others who share their view of the world but can also quickly become bored, especially with those who go into too much detail or who offer an alternative point of view. They are often quite sure that their way is right and can be difficult to persuade otherwise.

Warning!

These people may seem to some others to be rather arrogant, pushy and self-centred. But they are very driven and have the vision and the capability to achieve a lot.

Motivation type 3: Analytical-Autonomous

For these people, the main motivation in building relationships is to protect their own freedom and sense of independence. They usually feel better when things are structured and under control. Their communication style in first meetings may be reserved. Keeping quiet is their way to maintain a sense of autonomy and to show respect for the independence of others. In discussions they may take more time to think about things than others and may prefer to focus on more familiar and practical topics rather than discussing subjects that they know little about. They may be good at discussing and analysing details, but less engaged when it comes to more creative brainstorming.

Warning!

These people may come across to some others as too quiet, or even defensive, uninterested and critical of others. Yet one of their main aims is to allow other people space, out of their respect for their independence.

Motivation type 4: Flexible-Connecting

For these people, the main motivation in building relationships is learning, and they are ready to be very flexible in order to learn from and about others. They see themselves as curious, open to change and ready to compromise in relationships. They are happy to adapt their behaviour to manage complex situations. In first meetings they try to 'fit in' and to adapt to whatever others wish to talk about and do. They will show interest in other people's points of view to demonstrate this. They often have a group focus and will work to create harmony between group members.

Warning!

These people may seem to some others as difficult to judge, lacking direction, possibly very political, and too changeable. But they are also very open, sometimes highly creative, and very helpful in creating a positive group dynamic.

Managing first contacts

There are many different types of first meeting, from an unplanned greeting in an office corridor to an organised event such as a project kick-off meeting. Here we look at how to manage six different phases of a first meeting, remembering that we have to adapt our approach to each specific individual, business and cultural context.

Many people now work as part of a virtual team with team members spread across the globe (see Unit 15). There are fewer opportunities to get to know people and their work situations, and misunderstandings can easily arise. In such situations, it is essential to get as much advantage as possible from face-to-face meetings, in order to build mutual understanding and respect.

Phase 1: Preparing the ground

There are three stages in good preparation:

1 Research

Find out about the person you are going to meet. Use the internet or intranet, and talk to colleagues or other contacts to get background information on the person's outlook, experience, competence and current priorities.

2 Pre-meeting contact

You might send an email before you meet a new contact to 'break the ice' and to create a positive atmosphere for your face-to-face meeting.

3 Focus

Prepare to focus completely on the person when you meet them, giving them your full attention. Things will start well if you show interest in and respect for the person right from the start. First impressions count.

Phase 2: Introducing yourself

Personal introductions generally involve a spoken element (giving your name and / or origin: *I'm Mrs Li from the Shanghai office*) and a non-verbal component, for example, bowing or shaking hands.

Before you introduce yourself, decide which name or names to use, for example, your first and / or your family name. Always say your name slowly and clearly so others can hear how it is pronounced. It can be very helpful to give your business card at the same time so that your counterpart can read your name. If your name is long, or could be difficult to pronounce, it will help if you offer a simpler form: *Please call me* …. Your contact may also wish to hear an academic or job title such as Doctor or Head of Finance.

When working internationally, find out about protocols of role and hierarchy: who starts the introductions, and who introduces people to each other. The most senior person may have to handle the introductions. Also find out whether there should be an exchange of gifts.

First meetings can be a particular challenge for non-native speakers who do not feel so confident about their English. If you do feel more comfortable, you can be proactive and introduce contacts to each other, for example, *Oleg, have you met Touria?*

Phase 3: Starting small talk and developing the conversation

A host can start a conversation by asking about travel and offering refreshments before moving into the next phase of talking about different personal and professional topics. You can develop a conversation in many different ways, depending on the person in front of you. But you need to find the right topic. One way to do this is to:

1 look for a subject to talk about

2 develop the topic with follow-up questions

3 find things you have in common in order to create mutual understanding.

There are examples of the language you can use for each of these phases in the *What do you say?* section at the end of the unit.

To find the right topic, you can ask some exploratory questions on basic subjects such as travel, home, food and work. Some people like to talk about their last holiday. Others want to keep strictly to business topics. Focus on a topic that the other person seems to respond well to. And be sensitive to the pace of the conversation. Some people are much more comfortable with silence than others.

Remember also that people think and talk about the same topic in different ways. For example, when talking about holidays, some people like to give ideas about places to visit. Others like to talk about prices, or how to reach a destination. Whatever people are interested in, try to share similar experiences or opinions.

Your aim here is to establish rapport, which Wikipedia defines as 'a commonality of perspective, or being on the same wavelength as the person you are talking to'. Rapport involves people establishing a positive relationship and mutual understanding, leading to similar behaviour and shared thinking. Indeed, psychological research shows that people sharing rapport may move in the same way, share a common body language, and communicate with the same physical 'rhythm'.

Lunch for two: Small talk strategies to get the conversation going

Look at the following conversation between two colleagues having lunch during an international project meeting. How many small talk strategies can you identify in this conversation? Compare your answers with those in the answer key.

Jean: *So, Sam, how's the project going?*

Sam: *Fine, thanks, Jean. Everything's on schedule at the moment.*

Jean: *Excellent. No problems with the software installation?*

Sam: *We had a few questions at the start but nothing serious. How about your work?*

Jean: *We've finished.*

Sam: *Finished? Great. You must be pleased.*

Jean: *Absolutely. It was a tough project.*

Sam: *Yes, I can imagine. Still, we'll have to find you something else to keep you busy, Jean!*

Jean: *Yes, thanks very much for that thought. Shall we order?*

Phase 4: Getting down to business

The length of the small talk phase varies according to the preferences of the people involved. In some cultural contexts, it may be important to invest hours, days or even weeks in the process of getting to know each other. In more task-oriented environments, it may only take a few minutes before people get down to business. Whatever the context, it is critical that the bridge from small talk to business takes place in a way that everyone feels comfortable with. A standard way to manage this is to say *Shall we get down to business now?*

Phase 5: Saying goodbye

Once your business has been concluded, it is time to say goodbye. Some people indicate this moment by using words such as *Right* or *OK*, followed by a pause. They may also signal this physically by, for example, putting all their papers away or starting to look at their mobile phone.

But cultural, linguistic and personality factors may make it quite difficult to know when someone wants to end a conversation. Hesitation and silence could simply indicate that your contact is trying to remember a word. Asking questions such as *What are your plans for the rest of the day?*, *Are you going back to the hotel?* or *Shall I call a taxi for you?* can help to find out whether the other person wants the conversation to end.

As the conversation finishes, it may be important to use an explicit and positive statement such as *It was good to see you* or *I think that was a useful meeting*. You can also refer to a future event by saying *See you next month* or *I'll call you next week*.

Phase 6: Follow up

Relationships are not made in first meetings. They take time and commitment to develop in follow-up meetings and by email (see Units 10 and 11). Choosing which individuals to build stronger relationships with is part of networking and is examined in the next unit. How to move to a deeper level of trust is examined in Unit 5.

Relationships and gender

American linguistics professor Deborah Tannen writes about the communication styles of men and women. She believes that men and women manage relationships and social conversation in quite different ways. Although there are great dangers in over-generalising, and although the context in which she is working is North American, it is interesting to reflect on what Tannen has to say, and on how far our own behaviour and the behaviour of people we know conforms to these stereotypes.

Tannen argues that, for women, conversations are about establishing connections and negotiating relationships. Women express friendship by telling each other what they are feeling and what happened during the day. The emphasis is on finding similarities and matching experiences.

On the other hand, Tannen argues that, for men, talking is primarily a way to maintain independence and to negotiate and maintain status within the social order. The focus for men, who often compete to hold centre stage, is on demonstrating knowledge and skills, or simply on giving important information.

Because the two world views which she describes are so far apart, both sides can feel frustration when dealing with the other. These are some of the areas of possible misunderstanding:

1 Asking for help

Women may be more likely to ask questions when they need help. Men may view asking questions as showing a lack of knowledge and competence, and as a sign of weakness.

2 Offering support

Tannen suggests that men may feel worried by offers of support. They may interpret such offers as a suggestion that they are not competent to do a job independently. Women, on the other hand, may view offers of support more as gestures of solidarity and intimacy.

3 Discussing problems

Women discuss problems not necessarily to find solutions but to share feelings and to be listened to. When men hear about problems, they are quick to offer solutions and may not understand why women react negatively to advice.

4 Building arguments

According to other research findings, many women support their opinions during discussions with examples or cases from their personal experience. Their male colleagues often see these arguments as too subjective.

Test your relationship-building skills

The Centre for Intercultural Learning at the Canadian Foreign Service Institute defines a number of relationship-building skills for those working across cultures. Look at the checklist below based on the Centre's research. How far do you use these skills in your international working? Rate yourself from 1 (the lowest mark) to 7 (the highest).

An interculturally effective person ...   Score 1–7

1 has a relationship-building strategy
   – makes an effort to socialise with individuals from other cultures (will arrange meetings with individuals and find time to meet the wider communities in other cultures at every opportunity)
   – does not spend too much time abroad with fellow expatriates
   – does not become isolated from other cultures

2 has a language strategy
   – invests time in learning the local language when abroad and can manage simple phrases and some basic conversation
   – will regularly ask for translations or the meanings of words in the local language

3 knows other cultures
   – is able to describe key social protocols and codes of other cultures which are different from the home culture
   – is able to assess the importance of relationships and style of relationship building in other cultures

4 is sensitive to stereotypes
   – understands how people from their home culture may be viewed in other cultures
   – is able to avoid stereotypical thinking about people from other cultures which could lead to negative judgements

5 knows how he/she is seen in other cultures
   – will ask for feedback on his/her behaviour to check that it is appropriate for other cultures
   – will get positive feedback from international colleagues that he/she is friendly and fits well into other cultures

Total

Developing your skills

If you score lower than 5 in any of the above dimensions (or less than 50 overall), you should think about how you can build upon your strengths and also how you can improve in the areas where you are not so strong.

Results or relationships

Professionals who wish to be successful at work need to focus both on results and relationships. How far do you think you get the balance right?

What do you say?

Introducing yourself

• Good morning. My name is …	Nice to meet you. I'm …
• You must be …	That's right. Good to meet you.
• Welcome to …	Thank you. It's great to be here.
• This is Jan. He's responsible for …	Pleased to meet you.

Starting small talk

Offers

• May I take your coat?
• Please, take a seat.
• Would you like something to drink? Tea? Coffee? Juice?
• Can I get you something to drink?

Travel

• Did you have a good trip?
• How was the flight? Was everything on time?
• Did you have any problems finding us?
• Is everything OK with the hotel?
• Where are you staying?

Developing the conversation (1): Looking for a subject

Work

• Where are you based?
• What are you working on at the moment?
• How's business at the moment?
• Are you busy with the Telcom project? I heard it's going well.
• How is the reorganisation going? I heard it's a tough process.

People

• You know John Hansen, don't you? How is he?
• Have you heard anything about Jean-Claude?
• Is Hitashi still working with you in the project?

The schedule

• Would you like to meet for dinner tonight?
• Are you free tonight? I could show you …
• Would you like to join us this evening?

Travel

• Is this your first time in …?
• Do you travel a lot on business?

- *Have you been travelling much this year?*
- *How much travel do you do?*
- *Have you ever been to …?*

Country
- *Do you live in Santiago?*
- *Are you from there originally?*
- *So what's happening in … at the moment? I heard on the news that …*

Food
- *Would you be happy to eat Italian food tonight or would you like something else?*
- *Do you cook?*

Interests
- *Do you like …?*
- *Do you do any sport?*
- *Are you keen on …?*

Developing the topic (2): Asking open questions

- *When will you …?*
- *Why did you …?*
- *How do you …?*
- *What are you …?*

Using their words

Use words which others say during a conversation as a basis for follow-up questions or comments. Look at the different ways in which you can follow up a simple sentence which someone says during a conversation by exploring the words 'meeting' and 'Tokyo'.

I went to a meeting in Tokyo.

Ask about purpose	*What was the meeting about?*
Ask about results	*Was it a good meeting?*
Ask about people	*Was it a board meeting?*
Ask about timing	*How long did it last?*
Ask about location	*Where was the meeting? At the head office?*
Ask about frequency	*How often do you have to go to Tokyo?*
Ask about likes	*Do you like Tokyo?*
Ask about afterwards	*What did you do after the meeting?*

Developing the conversation (3): Finding things you have in common

- *So, you also …*
- *Did you have the same experience?*
- *How did you find it? Was it similar?*
- *Your background is IT? Mine too. What kind of IT work do you do?*

Getting down to business: Starting the meeting

- *I think we can get straight down to business if that's alright with you.*
- *We have a lot of things to get through today. Let's get started.*
- *We need to take some important decisions today. Shall we start?*

Saying goodbye

Time to go
- *Oh, I think my taxi has arrived.*
- *I'm afraid I'll have to go. I need to be up early tomorrow.*
- *I need to be at my next meeting at …*

Positive comments
- *It was good to meet you.*
- *Thanks for a very nice evening last night.*
- *I think we have made a lot of progress.*

Future contacts
- *We'll look forward to seeing you next month.*
- *I'll send you an email next week with the information.*
- *See you soon.*

Final comments
- *Goodbye.*
- *Have a good trip back. Bye.*
- *Take care.*

4 Networking

> **We are caught in an inescapable network of mutuality, tied in a single ... destiny. Whatever affects one directly, affects all indirectly.**
>
> Martin Luther King, American Baptist minister and civil rights leader (1929–68)

Many people think their networking skills are not good enough. This is strange because most people understand that developing a network of relationships is a key success factor in business.

So what stops people from networking? Some individuals feel uncomfortable approaching strangers, and in some business cultures it may be usual to maintain a professional distance from others. Others simply say they do not have enough time for networking (which means that they do not *make* enough time for it).

Also, many people do not fully understand the processes of networking. Obviously, if people do not know how to network, then they will not do it enough.

In this unit we present some guidelines for a very proactive style of networking, and look at how such an approach can help to develop your performance and that of others to deliver measurable business results. Before you read on, think about these questions:

1 What are the main benefits of networking?

2 Which people do you include in your network?

3 What conversational skills do good networkers have?

4 How can you make your networking deliver results?

The four Ps of proactive networking

There are four key principles to think about when you are building a network.

1 Purpose

The purpose of networking is to deliver tangible business benefits, for you or for your organization. Networking is about developing the right kinds of relationship with the right kinds of people. It can enable information to flow more efficiently inside an organisation. But remember it should be handled with integrity, and it should support the ethical principles of your organisation.

Because the purpose of networking is to get better business results, you should think carefully about your aims. Do you want to create a network that generates sales? Do you want to create job opportunities for yourself? Do you want to increase your influence within your organisation in order to promote and support your projects?

Defining a clear purpose will help you to give focus to your networking activities. This does not mean that you will necessarily see the results of your networking quickly or easily. But it is still a networking principle to have clear objectives and to regularly track your progress towards these objectives.

2 People

There are two main approaches to networking, which we can call 'hunting' and 'fishing'.

'Hunting' people is a targeted approach and involves defining carefully who we want to connect with, identifying where they can be found, and finding ways to get introduced, for example, by getting an invitation to a special event, offering to speak at one, and so on.

'Hunting' has clear benefits but also risks. We should in principle focus on key people and create a core network. But organisations are complex, and key decision-makers are not always easy to identify. Changes in company strategy can also suddenly bring us into contact with new parts of the organisation.

So it can be advantageous to go 'fishing' instead. This involves casting our net as widely as possible, and helping opportunities to arise more than creating them directly. It means making contact with people even when there is no obvious immediate benefit, for example, by talking to visitors passing through your office or spontaneously joining a group for lunch.

There may be tangible gains to this approach: unforeseen business opportunities may come your way. But there are also intangible advantages: this kind of 'seeding' can build your reputation as someone who is competent, experienced and nice to be with. This is something you can use when a specific need arises.

3 Perspective

People often do not invest enough time in networking because they have the wrong perspective. Successful networkers recognise that the people side of business is important, that you cannot succeed alone, and that you need others to give you information and support. Once you see this, you will start to give the necessary time and energy to building your network.

But giving time is not enough. A lot of people think about their networks in the wrong way. If you only think about what you can get from other people, they will soon start to feel that they are being used and will drop away, possibly damaging your reputation as they go. Networking should be seen as a way of delivering *mutual* benefits. This has a big impact on how you communicate with the people in your network.

4 Patience

Relationships do not develop overnight. Networking is much more than a quick handshake at a social event. It demands effort over the medium and long term. Relationships have to be looked after and encouraged to grow. Successful networkers have the patience to wait for results.

Using conversation to network

Networking is about having lots of good conversations with lots of people. So the first challenge is to create opportunities for such conversations to take place. Both direct and indirect approaches are possible.

A direct approach could be to set up a lunch or dinner meeting by asking a contact you have identified. An indirect approach may involve making requests such as *Would it be possible to meet your head of sales?*

Different people choose different approaches. If you feel comfortable about marketing yourself, you may prefer the direct approach. On the other hand, the cultural context may not always permit this. An indirect approach may work better if an intermediary can really help you to set up a meeting with the person you want to talk to.

Unplanned opportunities for conversation arise every day: in the company restaurant or canteen (where you decide to sit affects who you meet); at large meetings (which group you join for a coffee affects who you talk to); or in the corridors as you pass groups of colleagues talking. In all these situations, it helps to be a good reader of group dynamics.

1 Conversation and group dynamics

When good networkers enter a room, they can quickly assess who is available for conversation and who is in a closed dialogue which should not be interrupted. *Networking Like a Pro: Turning Connections Into Contacts*, by Misner, Alexander and Hilliard, contains useful guidance on how to deal with this kind of situation.

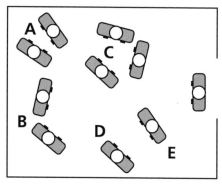

Conversation and group dynamics

You have just entered a room full of strangers having coffee before the start of a business seminar. (You are on the right in the diagram here.) Which of the groups of people (A–E) can you approach and engage in conversation? Refer to the answer key for the answer.

2 Breaking the ice

Once you have identified an individual or a group to talk to, you need to be able to approach and engage the other person or people in conversation.

What you say to break the ice depends, first of all, on whether you are introducing yourself to new contacts or meeting people who know you. There are no golden rules, only a number of options to consider, depending on your sense of the particular person and of the context. Take a look at the two approaches in this table. Which of these would you be happy to use?

The 'hard' approach	
• Connect quickly and explicitly to the other person's network. • Show knowledge of the person. • Highlight the reason for the conversation.	*Hello, I'm Lorenza Brunello. I've worked with a colleague of yours, Peter Pilger, and he said it would be good for us to meet as we're both running projects in China.*
The 'soft' approach	
• Focus on the immediate context. • Stay 'off topic'. • Identify common interests.	*Enjoying the conference? I've just been to a session on projects in China. I found it really fascinating since I'm having a few problems there with my own project.*

3 Managing conversations

Effective networkers need to do the basics well: speaking clearly and listening effectively (see Units 1 and 2). However, there are added dimensions to speaking and listening for networking purposes.

Speaking

Networkers need to do three things when speaking:

1 To be interesting. Good networkers are memorable and engaging. They have interesting stories and anecdotes with useful facts and figures. They show self-confidence. They want the listener to remember what they say and to want more.

2 To offer value. Good networkers provide information, insights and possible contacts that are useful in some way to the listener: *Would you like me to send you a copy of that report?* Networkers make themselves useful for other people to know: *I could help you with that if you want.*

3 To build rapport. Good networkers focus on things that the speaker and listener have in common. They communicate facts and feelings as a way of building openness and trust.

How good are your speaking skills for networking? Think about your answers to these questions:

- Which of my life experiences will engage others? Why is this so?
- What are my views on doing business successfully? What can others learn from me?
- What have I learned from others in my network that I can pass on?

Listening

Effective listening for networking is based on concentrating, and on asking questions to identify business opportunities. As you ask your questions, take mental notes about the person's background, motivation and needs. Then think about ways in which you might be useful to them and ways in which they might be useful to you. Look at the topic areas in the table on page 48 and think of some questions you could ask for each one. Then compare your answers with the ones in the *What do you say?* section at the end of this unit.

Listening for different topics

Topic	What you are listening for
Job and company	Identify overlaps of responsibility and challenge between you and them which could signify mutual interest.
Professional experience	It is important to get the bigger picture of the person – what are their values and attitudes?
Existing networks	Who do they know? How influential are they?
Approach to networking	Are they politically intelligent? Does networking turn them off?

4 Closing and following up

Effective networkers are good at finishing conversations on a positive note: *It was really good to meet you and to discuss the project.* Good networkers also focus on next steps: *I'll send you that information.* But if you promise to do something for the other person, then do make sure that you do it! Empty promises will damage your reputation.

After each networking conversation, you need to decide whether to keep the contact in your network. If so, keep a summary of who they are, how they can be useful to you, and how you can help them. Write down key professional and personal facts about the person as soon as you get an opportunity, for example, on the back of their business card, and then convert this into a longer summary, which you can keep in a database. An example of such networking notes is given below. How do your networking notes compare to these?

> Peter (call him Pete) is director of HR at Swedish Telia. Late 40s. Responsible for talent management. Strong international experience: worked in China for two years. Interested in support to develop an international leadership concept but not a great fan of intercultural training. Lives in centre of Stockholm Loves football: contact him next time Sweden plays. Action: Send a short summary of ideas and call him by end of June. He's open to a visit in autumn.

If people are worth contacting, then send an email within a week of the first meeting. If you use social networking sites (such as Linked-in or Xing), invite people to add you to their network. When you contact them, make sure that you include a reference to when you met, mention something positive about the meeting, and offer a clear benefit to the recipient and a proposal for future contact, as in this example:

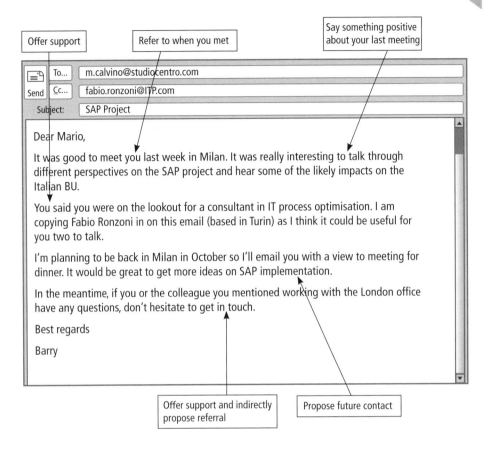

Offer support

Refer to when you met

Say something positive about your last meeting

To... m.calvino@studiocentro.com
Cc... fabio.ronzoni@ITP.com
Subject: SAP Project

Dear Mario,

It was good to meet you last week in Milan. It was really interesting to talk through different perspectives on the SAP project and hear some of the likely impacts on the Italian BU.

You said you were on the lookout for a consultant in IT process optimisation. I am copying Fabio Ronzoni in on this email (based in Turin) as I think it could be useful for you two to talk.

I'm planning to be back in Milan in October so I'll email you with a view to meeting for dinner. It would be great to get more ideas on SAP implementation.

In the meantime, if you or the colleague you mentioned working with the London office have any questions, don't hesitate to get in touch.

Best regards

Barry

Offer support and indirectly propose referral

Propose future contact

Networking – a two-way process

Networking is a process that takes time, planning, a lot of patience, and a degree of faith. You will often not see immediate results. To get things moving, you have to be proactive and offer support to others, encouraging them to then support you. You can offer support, for example, by volunteering to help with tasks, putting people in touch with an expert who can help solve a problem they have, emailing them a useful article, recommending an interesting conference, or even finding a project you can work on together.

How many times have you done any of these things with your network contacts in the last month? If you cannot remember, then you have just identified your first task for the next few days. Good luck!

What do you say?

The 'hard' approach

Connect to the other person's network
- *Hello, I'm Lorenza Brunello. I've worked with a colleague of yours, Peter Pleuger.*
- *Maria told me a lot about you.*

Show knowledge of the person
- *As I understand, you're responsible for sales in the Asia zone. Is that right?*
- *I've heard that your project is going very well.*

Highlight reasons for the conversation
- *Peter said it would be good for us to meet as we're both running projects in China.*
- *I'm keen to meet anyone with experience of implementing SAP in China.*

The 'soft' approach

Focus on the immediate context
- *Are you enjoying the conference?*
- *Would you like some more coffee?*

Stay 'off topic'
- *So do you have a busy afternoon today?*
- *Are you staying long?*

Identify common interests
- *I've just been to a session on projects in China. I found it really fascinating since I'm having a few issues there with my own project.*
- *So do you also work quite a lot with outsourcing?*

Asking questions as a networker

Topic	What you are listening for	Sample questions
Job and company	Overlaps of responsibility and challenge which could signify mutual interest	*So, what do you do? What are your main areas of responsibility?*
Professional experience	Important to get the bigger picture of the person – what are their values and attitudes?	*What's your background? Why did you move into ...?*
Existing networks	Who do they know? How influential are they?	*Do you know ...? Have you worked with ...?*
Approach to networking	Are they politically intelligent? Does networking turn them off?	Is the project challenging politically? Do you spend a lot of time at events like this?

Speaking as a networker

Deliver interest
- *Can I tell you a story I heard about ...?*
- *That reminds me of ...*

Offer value
- *It may be interesting for you to know that ...*
- *Maybe you should meet ... I can put you in contact.*

Build rapport
- *That's very interesting. I also had that experience when I ...*
- *I was also worried / concerned / anxious / confident / pleased / disappointed / ...*

Ending networking conversations

Finish on a positive note
- *It was really good to meet you.*
- *Thanks for the contact in Barcelona.*

Promise a future contact
- *I'll be in touch with information on change management for you.*
- *I'll give you a call next week to discuss the situation which we have in Thailand.*

Offer to refer
- *Shall I ask Paul to give you a call when I get back to the office?*
- *Do you want me to ask Kim to contact you?*

Emailing to follow up a networking meeting

The content and style of an email to follow up a networking meeting will depend on its objective and the level of relationship established. The following four-part structure can be used when you wish to offer support first as a gesture of goodwill to begin the relationship.

Refer to the meeting
- *It was good to see you at the project kick-off this week.*
- *Nice meeting you yesterday evening.*

Say something positive about your last meeting
- *It was good to learn more about how things work in Spain.*
- *The talk you gave was very interesting and relevant to my work here in the UK.*

Offer support / Propose referral
- *I'll ask Jon Dyson to call you as he may be able to help with some of the translation issues you mentioned.*
- *I've mentioned you to my boss and he'll be in touch in the next few days.*

Propose a future contact
- *Hope to see you next month in Milan.*
- *It would be great to talk more at our next monthly meeting.*

5 Building trust

You must trust and believe in people, or life becomes impossible.

Anton Chekhov, Russian short story writer, playwright and
physician (1860–1904)

If you ask business people for the essential ingredient that enables teams and
organisations to perform excellently, you will often get a one-word answer – 'trust'.

Without trust, expensive controls are needed to check on staff, information does not
flow freely, and motivation is lower. With trust in place, people have the freedom to fulfil
their roles, and to provide the cooperation and support to others to help them to reach
their goals too.

In this unit we look at some of the key dimensions of trust, using research by the
organisation, WorldWork. We also look at how you can increase trust within your team
and organisation. Before reading on, think about these questions:

1 What is trust?

2 What makes people trust each other?

3 Which communication strategies can help to develop trust?

4 What can make it difficult to develop trust in organisations?

What is trust?

This question is not easy to answer. First, we need to remember that trust is not optional. It is mandatory, and for one simple reason: because we cannot do everything ourselves. I trust others to fly the planes and drive the trains I travel in. I trust my IT department to configure my desktop PC correctly. We have to trust other people.

Fundamentally, trust involves interdependence. It means being confident that other people will meet our positive expectations: to drive our new car carefully, to deliver a work report on time, etc. The downside is that we put ourselves at risk, since someone could betray our trust. The upside is that we can take decisions: to get on the plane, and to plan our working week in the knowledge that the report will be delivered on time. Trust allows us to organise our lives and to get things done.

There are different kinds of trust, which operate at different emotional and intellectual levels. The relationship-based trust we place in family members or partners is very different from the professional trust we may place in colleagues, or the more impersonal trust we may place in institutions such as airlines, banks, governments and religious bodies.

Trust is also situational. We may trust a particular person in one situation but not in another. I might trust you to stand in for me in a meeting, but I might not trust you to drive my new car.

Building trust at work

What does all this mean for building trust at work? What factors make us have faith in some people but not in others? If we understand these factors, we may be able to speed up the process of building trust. Here we look at seven factors that can support the development of trust:

1 People trust those who are competent

This is so obvious that we may overlook it, but we are unlikely to trust others unless we believe they have the necessary skills. Estimating someone's competence may sometimes be based on relatively superficial factors, for example, the wearing of a particular uniform – as in the case of pilots, doctors or the police – may be enough in some situations to create trust. At work, a title or job function may be enough. But for our faith in others to continue over time, we normally need proof that someone has the relevant competence and the judgement to use it properly. Trust in the workplace often has to be earned.

Tips for building competence-based trust

- At work, people need to understand and appreciate each other's skills and talents. Some teams create a 'team book', in which they record their backgrounds for everyone to read. Other teams hand round people's resumés (or CVs) or encourage members to discuss their professional experience and skills over dinner.
- Colleagues need to be given a chance to prove themselves and show that they can be trusted. For leaders, this means delegating responsibility. Also, as team members succeed, it is important to celebrate success, so that competence is recognised and higher levels of trust can be developed.
- It is important to communicate your trust in other people's competence. Communicating about trust helps to create a trust culture.

2 People trust those who are similar to them

We tend to instinctively trust what is known and similar, and distrust what is different. We are more likely to have faith in people who have the same background, approaches, values, interests and objectives as us. This is important to recognise when working across cultures. There can be unnecessary levels of suspicion when people with different values and working practices meet because it is easy to misinterpret others' behaviours. So it is vital to invest time in getting to know other people in order that we can understand and appreciate them more.

Tips for building similarity-based trust

- Encourage people to ask questions about each other's backgrounds, interests, CVs and experience in order to find similarities. They can then discuss how these may help to improve the team's performance.
- Deal with any distrust that may arise between individuals from different backgrounds. Encourage a positive attitude to diversity. If you hear negative judgements, challenge these and focus people back towards collaboration based on common experiences and goals.

3 People trust those who show empathy

We are more likely to trust people whom we believe have our best interests at heart. It is much more difficult to trust someone whom we think wants to hurt us in some way.

Tips for building empathy-based trust

- Take an interest in the lives of colleagues. See it as part of your responsibility to understand their professional and personal priorities and the pressures they are under.
- Show them that they are important to you. Communicate your readiness to help them.
- Be an advocate for others. Show understanding when people have problems managing their workload. As a leader, you may be able to take on more yourself, or to delegate to others to reduce the pressure on someone who needs support.

4 People trust those with integrity

We generally respect and trust those who are honest, who keep their promises, and whom we think act according to a just moral code. We trust team-oriented people who work for the group more than those who seem mainly interested in furthering their own careers.

Tips for building integrity-based trust

- Communicate clearly about ethics. If you are a leader, try to build a team culture explicitly around defined values. Make clear when you can and when you cannot be open: some management information will be confidential and cannot be shared with team members. If you discuss openly the question of what you can and cannot tell other people, they will respect your judgement when you do feel the need to hold back information. This helps to build rather than damage trust.
- It is easy to say that you are going to be a fair, honest and team-oriented leader. But you must make sure that you really are all these things and that people recognise this.
- Give positive feedback and / or rewards.
- Encourage those who break the rules to respect the agreed values.

5 People trust those who are reliable

Trusting others, or getting others to trust us, is difficult if people are unreliable. You are more likely to be entrusted with a task if you have always demonstrated your reliability with the same kind of task in the past. People will find you more difficult to trust if you are unpredictable.

Tip for building reliability-based trust

- This dimension of trust takes time to develop. You have to prove through your actions over time that you are reliable. This means that you keep your promises and act consistently. This is particularly important in the early phases of team interaction. In other words, practise what you preach.

6 People trust those who involve them

We are unlikely to trust someone who we believe is not telling us the full story. We are also unlikely to trust someone who seems to be reluctant to share their true feelings.

Tip for building involvement-based trust

- Involvement means circulating and sharing key information openly and proactively. But building trust is an emotional process as well as a rational and logical one. So it may be helpful to be open about your feelings as well as about the facts. Involving others in our feelings and showing an interest in theirs can help to develop greater trust.

7 People trust those who trust them

Trust creates trust. If we want people to trust us, it helps if they believe that we trust them. In other words, one of the best ways to develop trust in a team is to show trust in others, even before you really have enough information to do so. This can be risky, of course. People may let us down. But taking this kind of risk can speed up the process of building trust in a team.

Tips for showing trust

- Communicate often and openly the fact that you trust others, even if you are not 100 per cent confident of their ability.
- Be explicit about the fact that you want people to trust you.

The trust challenge

Creating trust can seem difficult in today's business world. Working virtually, working across cultures, and being involved in complex change processes can all make the task of building trust more challenging than in the past.

Increasingly, employees are sceptical of the word 'trust', especially when the word is used by managers in organisations where there is a lot of internal politics, misinformation and a mentality of self-preservation.

But trust is essential. By talking about trust in your team or organisation, and developing a trust strategy, it is possible to achieve not only better relationships but also better performance.

What do you say?

Building competence-based trust

Talking about levels of competence
- *What's your background? Are you a specialist in …?*
- *What's your experience of international projects?*

Delegate to allow individuals to prove their competence
- *Could you …?*
- *Could you take responsibility for …?*

Celebrate high competence levels and excellent performance
- *Manfred did a great job in developing …*
- *I think the team is working really well together on …*

Communicate trust in other people's competence
- (More explicit) *No, I don't need to see the report before you send it. I trust your judgement on this.*
- (Less explicit) *Why don't you contact the customer directly, since you are good at doing this kind of job.*
- *I trust you to …*
- *I'm very happy for you to handle this.*

Building similarity-based trust

Ask questions to discover similarities
- *Have you ever worked in …?*
- *Do you think that we should …?*

Talk about similarities
- *I've also worked in …*
- *Me, too.*

Encourage a positive attitude to diversity
- *I think we need to see diversity as an opportunity.*
- *We have a good range of skills in the team.*
- *It's good to have different levels of experience and background in the team.*

Act against negativity
- *We need to support each other, not criticise each other.*
- *I don't think it's fair to blame Brian.*
- *This will be a challenge, but it can help us to think more creatively to reach our goal.*

Building empathy-based trust

Take an interest in the lives of colleagues
- *How are things going?*
- *Are you under a lot of pressure at the moment?*

Communicate the fact that you care
- *If you need any help, …*
- *Just ask me if you want some support with …*

Act as an advocate if others need defending
- *In Gudrun's defence, I think she was trying to …*
- *I think she wanted to …*

Show understanding when people have problems managing workload
- *I understand that you're under a lot of pressure.*
- *How can we help you finish this?*

Take on more yourself or delegate to others
- *Would you like me to …?*
- *Gudrun, could you do this for Mohamed to free him up a little?*

Building integrity-based trust

Build a team culture explicitly around defined values
- *I believe we need to respect certain values, like …*
- *We need to be honest with each other.*

Clarify when you can and when you cannot be open
- *I want to communicate openly about …*
- *But I can't communicate confidential information about …*

Make sure your actions follow the agreed values
- *In line with our values, I would like to …*
- *As I said at the start, honesty is important.*

Give positive feedback when values are respected
- *Thank you, Sue. It's important for us to be honest.*
- *I think this is a good example of what this team stands for.*

Encourage those who break the rules to respect core values
- *Peter, I think in future you need to …*
- *Inge, I don't think it's fair to the others to …*

Building reliability-based trust

Make clear the importance of reliability
- *We need to make sure we keep our promises.*
- *If you say you will do something, then please do it.*

Highlight your reliability when keeping your promises
- *As I promised, here is the report you wanted for the meeting tomorrow.*
- *As we agreed, I completed the project last week.*

Building involvement-based trust

Share data openly and proactively with others
- *Here is some information about the new project.*
- *I want to share this information …*

Be open with feelings as well as facts
- *My feeling is that …*
- *I'm worried / happy / confident that …*

Show trust

Communicate the fact that you trust
- *I have complete confidence in you to deliver on time.*
- *I'm sure we can trust them to …*

Communicate the fact that you can be trusted
- *You can rely on me to support you.*
- *Don't worry. I promise to …*

6 MAKING DECISIONS

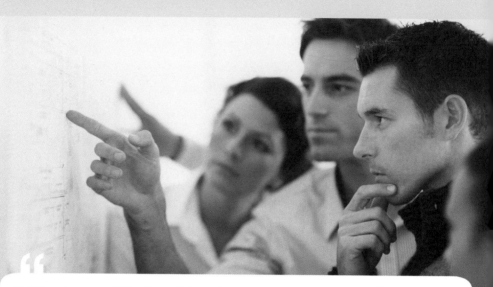

> **Nothing is more difficult, and therefore more precious, than to be able to decide.**
>
> Napoleon Bonaparte, Emperor of the French (1769–1821)

In this unit we look at how to make decisions in meetings. Effective decision-making requires different competences. These include:

- organisational skills (planning meetings)
- facilitation skills (managing the meeting)
- management skills (tracking decisions to ensure that actions are implemented).

We also give you the opportunity to profile your decision-making style and think about how effective it is with your international partners. Before you read on, think about these questions:

1 Why is business decision-making becoming more difficult?

2 How can you facilitate a discussion with a culturally diverse group?

3 What kind of decision-maker are you?

4 What is the best way to lead a decision-making meeting?

5 How can you ensure that decisions are taken and implemented?

Decision-making is getting more complex

Business used to be simpler. The working environment was less complicated, and information could be collected and analysed more easily. Big decisions came top-down from senior management, and were carried out by middle managers and the rest of the organisation.

Nowadays, business is international and the business environment is more complex and more ambiguous. This is why risk management is becoming more and more important. We often make decisions before we have all the information we need, and so these decisions have to be changed as we get more data.

The rise of the matrix organisation, with multiple reporting lines, means that a range of stakeholders can be involved in decision-making processes. The increasing cultural diversity of organisations also presents a challenge. Individuals from different departments and countries can enter a meeting with very different ideas about how it should be run and how decisions should be made.

Managing diversity in decision-making

Decision-making meetings can be run more effectively if the following questions have been answered and a clear and simple process has been agreed. There are different ways to get answers to these questions. It can be done collectively as part of the meeting itself, or handled in pre-meeting contacts between the leader and individual participants.

1 What is a decision?

For some people, a decision is a binding commitment. For others, it is simply a guideline and can be changed if the situation changes or if new information becomes available. For these people, the objective is to reach the best result, not to respect a past decision.

2 Who takes the decision?

For some people, decision-making is the responsibility of the leader. In more individualist cultures, people tend to think that individuals should take decisions in their areas of responsibility. Some people even feel that meetings reach better decisions if the leader is not present so that team members feel free to speak openly. In more collectivist cultures, people feel that the best decisions are reached when the whole group is involved. In more service-oriented cultures, customers may participate in decision-making because they are important stakeholders too.

3 How is a decision taken?

For some individuals, a structured decision-making process with a clear agenda and voting procedure is most effective. For others, it is better to be less systematic in order to be more creative. With some people, it is possible to speak very directly and yet still be polite, for example, *That's completely wrong, Hussein.* For others, a less direct approach is seen as the polite way to respect feelings, for example, *I understand what you're saying, Hussein. However, … .* Some people need to analyse risks in detail in order to avoid making a mistake. For others, it is better to take decisions quickly and then correct any mistakes that have been made.

4 Where is the decision taken?

For some people, it is better to hold meetings at an organisation's head office, and combine this with other meetings. For others, it is better to rotate the location of key decision-making meetings around regional offices in order to develop understanding of the different working contexts of team members. Also, while some people are happy to take decisions in virtual meetings, such as audio or video conferences, others find it essential to meet face to face.

5 How are people informed of decisions?

For some individuals, it is enough to send the minutes of the meeting, or a short email with an attached presentation to the relevant people, both participants and others. For others, it is better to inform those not at the meeting – team or department members and external customers and stakeholders – via a mix of face-to-face briefings and written communication.

There are no right or wrong answers here. What you do should depend on the outlooks and abilities of the people involved and the demands of the specific situation. People leading international meetings have to choose from the following **ABCDE** strategies to manage different expectations:

Adapt	Adapt your style to match the expectations of others.
Blend	Be flexible and mix different approaches together.
Co-create	Develop a new and unique meeting culture together.
Divide	Agree to do it 'my way' today and 'your way' next time.
Enforce	If necessary, use a 'pull' approach and tell people to do it 'my way'.

Your decision-making style

People take decisions in different ways, and Rowe and Boulgarides in their book *Managerial Decision Making: A Guide to Successful Business Decisions* have tried to classify these styles. They stress the importance of values, needs and preferences in understanding why individuals take decisions in the way they do. Their model describes four main decision-making styles, based on whether an individual is more task- or more relationship-oriented, and on how complex he or she wants the information to be on which they base decisions. The model shows us different motivations behind decision-making:

Complex	**ANALYTIC** Strong need for achievement (needs challenges)	**CONCEPTUAL** Strong need for achievement (needs recognition)
Information	**DIRECTIVE** Strong need for power	**BEHAVIOURAL** Strong need for affiliation
Simple		
	Task oriented	*People oriented*

1 Directive

Directive decision-makers need power. They are usually very results-oriented but also need to feel that they are in control of others or can dominate them. They are not very tolerant of ambiguity and prefer to keep things pragmatic and simple. They tend to take decisions based on less information and fewer alternatives. They like to work fast and to feel that it is their decision and not someone else's.

2 Analytical

Analytic decision-makers need to achieve. Being challenged motivates them. They are more tolerant of ambiguity than the 'Directives' and are also more comfortable handling information. This means that they can tolerate higher information loads and a greater number of possible courses of action, which they will analyse in detail over a longer period.

3 Conceptual

Conceptual decision-makers are also achievement-oriented but are less analytical in their thinking. They are comfortable with high information loads, but their people orientation means that their information collection methods may come through talking to people, especially to people who they see as experts. They tend to take a longer-term perspective and to be more creative than more analytical people.

4 Behavioural

Behavioural decision-makers have a strong people orientation. They generally communicate easily, using simple and understandable messages, and make efforts to express interest in the well-being of others. They consult a great deal, are open to suggestions, are happy to compromise, and prefer a looser sense of leadership control. They do not feel the need to own decisions; they prefer decisions to be owned by everybody.

Ask yourself

What kind of decision maker are you? What kind of decision-makers are your international partners? How far do you need to adapt your decision-making style to work more effectively with your international partners?

Leading decision-making meetings

There are four key stages in a decision-making meeting that you need to manage effectively.

1 Getting started

When people work together over longer periods, there is less need to explain what a meeting is and how it should work. But with culturally diverse teams, it is useful for the chairperson to adopt a more explicit and structured approach to ensure that the purpose of the meeting, and the decision-making process, are clear.

Stage in an introduction to a meeting

Look at the following extract from the start of a meeting. What can you identify as the main stages in this introduction (e.g. welcome, introduce agenda, . . .)? You can then refer to the answer key for the answer. How useful would this style of introduction be for your international meetings? What things would you say differently? Which of the main building blocks would you not use?

OK, shall we get started? First, a quick welcome to Jan, who has joined us from the Belgian office. Nice to have you here. Jan will be presenting some figures later when we talk about the new cross-border initiative. OK, in terms of agenda, if you all have it in front of you, as you can see, the main objective today is to take a decision on the next phase of the project. Do we feel ready to start, and, if so, when? We'll do an update of progress so far, that's from me. Then I just want to give you some information from the recent leadership meeting in Milan. And then we can talk about the decision, and the pros and cons of moving on with things now or waiting. Just to remind you of a few rules, as always: mobile phones off, and the native English speakers should try to speak clearly so that our colleagues from around the world can understand. OK? Good, then let's get started with . . .

2 Facilitating group discussion

Once the introductions are over, and the purpose and process have been clarified, the next challenge is to manage the discussion. 'Facilitation' refers to a set of communication techniques used to manage group discussions. The chairperson is usually seen as the facilitator, but the efficiency and effectiveness of the discussion can be improved a lot if everyone uses facilitation skills. Some international leaders like to use external facilitators so that they, as leaders, do not dominate and so risk reducing the creativity of their team.

There are a number of key tasks that the facilitator needs to perform:

Stimulate the discussion

The first step towards a decision is to encourage participants to think creatively about possible solutions. Questions are the key here, and there are a number of different types that can be used:
* Questions to suggest a process: *Can we brainstorm a few ideas to begin?*
* Questions to invite opinions: *Sylvie, what do you think?*
* Questions to evaluate ideas: *Which of these ideas is most interesting for us?*
* Questions to stimulate alternatives: *Can we have some other views on this?*
* Questions to check direction: *So what is our next step?*

Create the right atmosphere

The facilitator should manage the emotional temperature to support decision-making. Ideas flow faster when the atmosphere is good and people feel relaxed. Praise and positive feedback can be used to create a 'feel-good factor'. However, since the practice of feedback differs so much across cultures, facilitators need to use different styles to meet individual and cultural needs. Here are some examples with an explicitly positive feel:
* Using quality words (to satisfy feelings): *Thanks for that idea. It's a **great** suggestion.*
* Using process words (to satisfy the intellect): *Good. I think this has been very **efficient**.*

Clarify

It is often difficult for non-native speakers of English to follow and understand a complex discussion. The facilitator should ensure, as far as possible, that everything is clear for everyone. This can be done in two main ways:
* Focus on surface-level clarity. This means clarifying the meaning of what is said: *If I understand you correctly, you mean …*
* Focus on deep-level clarity. This means clarifying the motivation or assumptions behind the words: *Why do you say that? Do you feel that …?*

Good facilitators ask questions like these even when they themselves are sure of the answers, if they believe it helps others in the group.

Keep control

The facilitator has to watch the time. Reminding people of the agenda and pushing people to move on are also important functions, although it is necessary to be sensitive to the different priorities that people give to schedules.

Ensuring balanced participation – so that everyone has a chance to speak – is another part of the facilitator's role. Personality and cultural factors can affect the participation styles of different members: facilitators may need to work hard to encourage quieter, more introverted people to take part, and to make sure that talkative extroverts do not talk too much.

- Encouraging quiet people: *Harald, what do you think? It would be good to hear your ideas.*
- Controlling talkative people: *Sorry to interrupt, Valerie, but can we hear from Harald first, please?*

Summarise

Frequent summarising helps to create common understanding and provides opportunities to reflect and comment on what has been said and on the process. Some facilitators like to take responsibility for summarising. Others delegate this to group members who do it well. Allowing break-out groups for non-native speakers to summarise the meeting in their own language can also be helpful.

- Summarising the discussion: *So we have discussed a number of issues today.*
- Summarising the process: *I thought the discussion was excellent at the beginning, but we must make sure that we listen carefully to everybody.*

3 Optimising diversity

International meetings can be very diverse in terms of general outlook (analytical / creative), attitudes to decision-making (hierarchical / egalitarian), communication styles (direct / indirect), language level, and so on. Facilitators can use these three strategies to deal with this challenge:

Norming

Defining a clear process and clear communication rules is one way to manage differences in attitude, communication style and language level. Examples of such rules are:

- Everyone should have the opportunity to say something at the meeting.
- The chairperson has the right to interrupt people who talk for too long.
- The chairperson should invite quieter individuals to say something.

Linking

This means asking individuals explicitly to comment on each other's ideas.
- Connecting ideas: *Andres, what do you think about Brittany's point?*
- Directing questions to the group: *Can I ask Anna to answer your question, Jan?*

Linking forces people to listen to each other and engage with their ideas. This can develop mutual understanding and respect, and create a sense of teamwork and commitment towards the common target.

Integrating

This means bringing together ideas to encourage a creative approach. It involves respecting different points of view, looking for compromise, and finding solutions by taking the best from the different perspectives.
- Identifying differences of opinion: *The major issue at the moment seems to be ...*
- Respecting different positions: *OK, I think both these opinions are useful.*
- Exploring compromise: *If we were to ..., could you ...*
- Taking the best from the diverse perspectives: *John, if we take your point on cost saving and what Louise said about customer priorities, we could ...*

Achieving synergy is the ultimate aim of facilitation. Diversity can seem to be a threat to group decision-making processes, but it also represents a great opportunity in terms of creativity and innovation.

4 Making the decisions

At some point, the talking has to stop and decisions have to be made. However, it can sometimes be difficult to move a group away from discussing ideas and towards actually taking a decision. Use these three steps:
1 Guide the discussion towards a decision.
2 Confirm the decision.
3 Agree who does what and by when.

Look at this extract from a meeting, in which you will see these three steps in action.

Fiona: *OK, we need to take a decision on this. We're running out of time. Marianne, do you agree to this?*

Marianne: *Yes.*

Fiona: *Good. And Frank, can you go with this?*

Frank: *Yes, that's fine with me.*

Fiona: *OK, this means we're deciding to open the new store at the end of the year, not in the middle as we originally planned. What we need to do now is look again at roles and scheduling. Marianne, what's your availability for the second half of this year? ...*

5 Closing and implementing

Despite all the hard work done to create a clear communication process and include everyone in the decision-making, many international meetings finish with participants unclear about what has been agreed, and they may be too embarrassed to admit this. Here is a six-step process for closing international meetings:

1 Confirm that all points have been discussed.
2 Summarise.
3 Check that the decisions are understood.
4 Repeat who is responsible for what and by when – make sure this is in the minutes.
5 Agree the date of the next meeting.
6 Close with positive comments on the outcome of the meeting.

Now read an extract from the close of a meeting. Which of the steps are included and which not? Notice how the chair makes positive comments about the success of the meeting. How important in your working context is it to celebrate success in this way?

OK, are there any other points we need to talk about today? No? Then perhaps I should sum up quickly and confirm the next steps. Basically, we've agreed to set up a pilot project to see if this is the right software for the company. And we've also suggested that Gill will head things up, although this needs to be confirmed with her line manager. The time frame for completion is open and that's something to be discussed at the next meeting – pretty urgently in fact. Then in terms of actions, I need to talk to my boss and see if we can get a budget for this. Once that is confirmed, we can get together and start to define the project teams and sub-projects in more detail. That's in the minutes, Bob, yes? Good. Right, then I think we can finish there. Let me close by saying: great job! It was a difficult meeting in many ways but a great result, and I feel there's real commitment to this from everyone. Thank you!

6 Managing and monitoring decisions

Decision-making really starts when the meeting stops. Effective international managers need to work hard to track the decisions taken in order to check that participants have understood them and are committed to doing what they said they would do. Without such tracking, the implementation of decisions will fall behind schedule as participants give time to other work priorities.

Think about what happens when decisions are made in your organisation. Are they always implemented as planned? What can you do to make sure you and others implement decisions effectively?

Decision-making styles

Differences in decision-making style can cause real challenges for professionals collaborating internationally. Take time to clarify how decisions will be taken, by whom and for what purpose. This will help you to work fare more effectively.

What do you say?

Stimulating the discussion by asking questions

Questions to suggest a process
- *Can we brainstorm a few ideas to begin with?*

Questions to invite opinions
- *Sylvie, what do you think?*

Questions to evaluate ideas
- *Which of these ideas is most interesting for us?*

Questions to stimulate alternatives
- *Can we have some other views on this?*
- *Is there another way to see this?*

Questions to check direction
- *So what is our next step?*

Creating the right atmosphere

Maintaining a positive perspective
- *I'm confident that we will …*
- *I'm sure we can find a solution to …*

Giving positive feedback
- *Thanks for that idea. It's a great suggestion.*
- *Good. I think this has been very efficient.*

Making people feel confident about speaking
- *No decision has been made so feel free to give your ideas.*
- *Just say what you think and then we can …*

Clarifying

Checking the meaning of what is said
- *If I understand you correctly, you think …*

Checking the motivation or assumptions behind the words
- *Why do you say that? Do you feel that …?*

Keeping control

Time-keeping
- *We're running short of time. I think we need to …*
- *Can we deal with that a little later and focus for the moment on …*
- *Can we move on to the next point on the agenda?*

Encouraging quiet people
- *Harald, what do you think? It would be good to hear your ideas.*

Controlling talkative people
- *Sorry to interrupt, Valerie, but can we hear from Harald first, please?*

Summarising

Ideas
- *If I understand you correctly, …*

Sections of discussion
- *So, we have discussed a number of issues today.*

The process
- *I thought the discussion was excellent at the beginning, but we must make sure that we listen to everybody.*

Stopping talkative speakers
- *So your main idea is …*

Asking for more detail
- *Can you say a little more about …?*

Optimising diversity

Norming
- *I'd like to propose a few guidelines for the meeting.*

Linking
- Connecting individuals' ideas: *Andres, what do you think about Brittany's point?*
- Directing questions back to the group: *Can I ask Anna to answer your question, Jan?*

Integrating
- Identifying differences of opinion: *The major issue at the moment seems to be …*
- Respecting different positions: *OK, I think both these opinions are important to think about.*
- Exploring compromise: *If we were to …, could you …?*
- Taking the best from the diverse perspectives: *John, if we take your point on cost saving and what Louise said about customer priorities, we could…*

Taking the decision

Guide the discussion towards a decision
- *Are we ready to take a decision?*
- *I think we need to take a decision.*

Confirm the decision
- *OK, this means we have decided to …*
- *Does everyone agree?*

Agree who does what and by when
- *Can we agree who is responsible for …?*
- *What is the deadline for this? Shall we say …?*

Closing an international meeting

Confirming that all points have been discussed
- *Are there any other points?*

Summarising
- *To summarise, we decided that …*
- *Let's summarise what we have decided.*

Checking that the decisions are understood
- *Is that OK for everyone?*
- *John, any final comments?*
- *Is there anything to clarify?*

Repeat who is responsible for what and by when
- *So, in terms of next steps, I will … by the end of …*

Agree the date of the next meeting
- *Can we schedule the next meeting? Shall we say …?*

Close with positive comments on the outcome of the meeting
- *Many thanks for today. I think we made good progress …*
- *See you all at the next meeting. I hope you all have a safe journey home.*

Tracking decisions

Checking status
- *Have you … yet?*
- *When are you planning to …?*

Clarifying delays
- *What's the reason for the delay?*
- *Do you need any support?*

Requesting an update
- *Can you let me know when you have managed to …?*
- *Just email me after you have …*

Email and meetings

Here are two sample emails to help you to think about how to plan and follow up on a decision-making meeting.

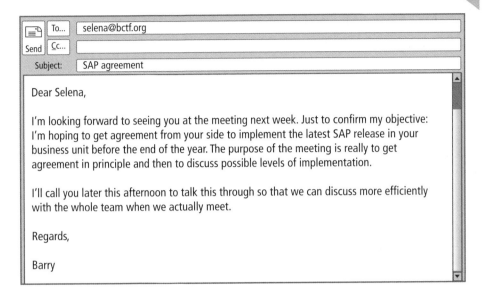

To... selena@bctf.org
Cc...
Subject: SAP agreement

Dear Selena,

I'm looking forward to seeing you at the meeting next week. Just to confirm my objective: I'm hoping to get agreement from your side to implement the latest SAP release in your business unit before the end of the year. The purpose of the meeting is really to get agreement in principle and then to discuss possible levels of implementation.

I'll call you later this afternoon to talk this through so that we can discuss more efficiently with the whole team when we actually meet.

Regards,

Barry

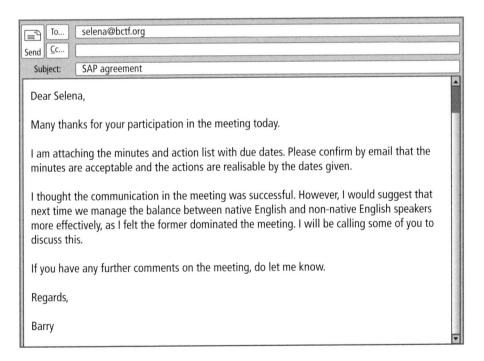

To... selena@bctf.org
Cc...
Subject: SAP agreement

Dear Selena,

Many thanks for your participation in the meeting today.

I am attaching the minutes and action list with due dates. Please confirm by email that the minutes are acceptable and the actions are realisable by the dates given.

I thought the communication in the meeting was successful. However, I would suggest that next time we manage the balance between native English and non-native English speakers more effectively, as I felt the former dominated the meeting. I will be calling some of you to discuss this.

If you have any further comments on the meeting, do let me know.

Regards,

Barry

7 INFLUENCING

> **Character may almost be called the most effective means of persuasion.**
>
> Aristotle, Greek philosopher (384–322 BC)

The ability to influence other people is a vital skill in business. But, as a result of organisational change, it is also becoming more challenging.

Professionals increasingly work in complex matrix structures with multiple reporting lines. They also work more and more in project teams for which the sponsor and project leader may be located in other countries. In these situations, both team members and leaders may find it more difficult than in the past to influence those with whom they work. To do so, they need new and smarter methods.

In this unit we look at some of the skills involved in influencing others, and provide some practical techniques for you to use at work in future. Before you read on, think about these questions:

1 What do you think are meant by the 'push' and 'pull' approaches to influencing?

2 Which influencing techniques are most effective for you?

3 How can you deal with people who say 'no'?

4 What is *personal branding* and how can you use it to influence your career development?

A question of power

Our ability to influence others depends on many factors. One of the most important is power. If we hold power over somebody, this greatly increases the chance that they will do what we want them to do.

Power can come from many sources. Many societies connect power to gender (usually, but not always, male) or age, with elders carrying more authority. In modern organisations, in spite of talk of empowerment, leaders keep the right to take most big strategic and operational decisions.

If you have power in a particular situation, you can use a 'push' approach. This involves telling someone what to do. Many purchasers enter negotiations with vendors using this approach, exerting pressure for lower prices and / or increased levels of service.

Most vendors, on the other hand, recognise their weaker position and use a 'pull' approach. This involves creative questioning and effective listening in order to identify mutual needs that can be satisfied via a 'win-win' solution.

Techniques for influencing people

As with all communication, influencing others has to be seen within a specific context. Something which persuades a person in one situation may fail totally in another. Here we look at eight dimensions of influencing others at work.

1 Stress the benefits

People are more likely to be influenced by someone who offers something that satisfies their interests. These interests may be tangible, such as a salary increase or a more interesting job. Or they may be less tangible, like recognition or appreciation. Successful influencers are like detectives who find out what others need and then satisfy these needs in a way that is seen as supportive, not patronising.

Ask yourself: How far do you focus on asking people questions to find out their needs rather than telling them what you 'know' is good for them?

2 Build trust

People are more likely to be influenced by someone they trust (see Unit 5). If I ask you to do something, and you trust that there is a good reason behind my request, there is a greater chance that you will agree. But how do we build trust? Three main ingredients in trust are:
• competence
• integrity
• empathy.

Showing these help you to build trust and, through this, to create opportunities to influence others.

Ask yourself: Do people know enough about you and your skills to trust in your judgement?

3 Be transparent

People who explain their thinking openly, and who get their ideas across clearly, are more likely to be seen as convincing. In contrast, people who have difficulty expressing their ideas, and who cannot explain effectively the reasons behind their suggestions, may be seen as incompetent, or even manipulative.

Ask yourself: How far are you seen to be a clear communicator?

4 Use logical arguments

People find it hard to resist an argument built on logic and solid data. However, it is important to communicate the right level of information and analysis when building an argument because very complicated arguments can threaten and confuse some people.

Ask yourself: How far do people describe you as someone who uses logical arguments (without being too complex)?

5 Focus on the relationship

People are usually more open to being influenced by people they like or with whom they have something in common. This makes relationship-building and networking skills important, so you should invest time in developing personal relationships. Remember, however, that the speed and style of relationship building depends on psychological and cultural factors (see Unit 4).

Ask yourself: Do you know how others view your attempts to influence them?

6 Be strong

People are more likely to be influenced by someone who communicates their ideas with energy and enthusiasm. If you do not seem convinced by your own arguments, why should others be? However, it is important to consider psychological and cultural factors here too. What is seen as powerful and assertive in some contexts could be seen as aggressive in cultures that value harmony.

Ask yourself: How far do others see the way you argue and persuade as being, on the one hand, assertive or, on the other hand, aggressive?

7 Look to the future

People who have a clear vision of the future, and who can explain clearly how they plan to realise this vision, are seen as more engaging and influential. Visions expressed in terms of a metaphor or story, rather than with facts and figures, may be more inspirational and effective.

Ask yourself: How far do others see you as inspirational and visionary?

8 Show optimism

Being negative is not usually inspiring. Positive thinkers, with energy and enthusiasm for creative solutions, are usually more appealing and influential. So try to persuade people by being more 'can do' than 'maybe not'. However, do not come across as being over-optimistic or over-positive, as people may see this as unprofessional.

Ask yourself: Do others see you as a positive or negative person?

Storytelling as an influencing technique

Storytelling is the most powerful way to put ideas into the world today.
Robert McAfee Brown, theologian and peace campaigner (1920–2001)

A growing number of business leaders are learning storytelling skills to help them to influence their employees. Storytelling is an ancient skill that has informed, entertained and influenced people for thousands of years. Traditionally, oral stories were a means of transferring culture from one generation to another, creating a bridge between past and present. Today, business leaders create memorable stories to inspire, influence and guide their employees through change, something that is often impossible with a simple explanation of facts and figures.

The use of personal anecdotes is one of the most common storytelling techniques. Anecdotes have the advantage of 'revealing' the human side of the leader, connecting speaker and listener at an emotional level, with the audience experiencing reality through the eyes, ears and feelings of the storyteller. Here are four different types of anecdote that you can use to influence people:

1 An insight into personal values

Telling a short story about yourself – for example, how you faced a difficult choice or an embarrassing moment, or how you achieved an important success unexpectedly – can be a good way to talk about shared personal values and establish a basis for others to know and respect you.

2 A learning experience

Sharing a learning experience, particularly if it is personal or even painful, can be a powerful way to support your proposals. Telling a story that shows how you initially made a mistake but then, with help, learned how to solve a problem similar to the challenge facing your organisation, is a powerful way of introducing a solution to a current problem.

3 A moment of confusion

Telling a story about a misunderstanding you once experienced – either because you misunderstood someone or because they misunderstood you – can be a good way to challenge people's perceptions of a situation, to warn them against misunderstanding, or to ask them to look more deeply into an idea that, at first sight, they would reject.

4 A tale of persistence

Telling a story of perseverance in the face of hardship and difficulty is a good way to raise spirits at difficult times and to motivate people to keep going. These stories tend to rely on anecdotes about famous historical or contemporary figures but can also work well if they touch on an element of your own life story.

Try it yourself

Use each of the four storytelling formats to develop personal anecdotes that you can use in a range of professional contexts to persuade others.

Dealing with 'no'

Your ability to influence others depends partly on your ability to prepare effective arguments. It also depends on your ability to deal with objections to your proposals, to be able to come up with effective responses when people say 'no' to your ideas. So try to anticipate objections and plan your counter-arguments. On page 79 are several types of objection that are commonly made in discussions. What counter-arguments can you use? Note down some ideas and compare your answers with those in the *What do you say?* section. Can you think of any other types of argument that you might hear?

Type of objection	What is said	How to respond
Morality	*That isn't ethical.*	
Analysis	*We need more data.*	
Experience	*We've tried this before.*	
Priorities	*I have something else to do.*	
Fear of failure	*What if this goes wrong?*	
Ignorance	*I don't understand.*	
Power play	*I cannot accept this.*	
Fear of change	*I think many people will react negatively to the change.*	

Influencing how people see you

Influencing people is not limited to single issues, such as getting agreement on an agenda point in a meeting. Influence has much wider importance, especially if we think about how we should build our reputation and career inside an organisation. Every time you walk into a room you create some kind of effect with the clothes you wear, your hairstyle, your smile, the way you speak and listen, the way you lead, and so on.

Some professionals find it helpful to think about their *personal branding*. There are consultancies which aim to help people to influence how they are seen by superiors, colleagues and clients in order to improve their career opportunities. Not everyone likes this approach, but if you decide to adopt it and try to interest others in your personal brand, you need both a clear product (what you are) and a promotional strategy (to make others aware of you). These three steps can help you to create your brand:

Step 1: Define your USP

Your Unique Selling Proposition (USP) consists of the special features you offer, your unique value. Brands such as Pepsi, Nike and BMW spend millions on their USPs, but you have to do it less expensively! So think about what you can offer that makes you different and valuable to the people around you at work. Use the questionionaire at the end of this section to help you to describe your special value to others. Then write down a short brand statement for yourself, using fewer than 20 words, and read it aloud to yourself several times. What does this really say about you? Do you think others think about you in the same way? If not, you have a selling job to do.

Step 2: Promote yourself

You may have wonderful qualities but if nobody in your organisation knows about them, then you are unlikely to maximise your potential. Successful branding is based on an effective communication strategy. This means promoting yourself internally to colleagues and management, as well as externally to customers. If you want to be seen to be valued, you need to take steps to become known – by getting invited to meetings, participating in extra projects, going to conferences, building new networks, and letting people know who you are and what you can do. The network that you build – friends, colleagues, clients and customers – will act as a promotional tool for your reputation and create career opportunities.

Step 3: Add value through visible leadership

If you want to improve the value of your career brand, you have to take the initiative and show leadership potential as often as possible. This can include everything from taking the minutes in weekly staff meetings to volunteering to lead new projects. As you acquire additional responsibilities, your authority and reputation will grow, adding further to your brand image.

Check your ability to influence

So, are you a successful influencer? How well are you doing? You probably have a sense of your own success, but do you ask people around you about this? Getting feedback is the best way to discover how successful an influencer you really are. So why not ask a few trusted superiors, colleagues or customers about your personal style of influencing people? What can they tell you about your performance in meetings or your style of presenting? Getting this information will enable you to identify the strengths you can work on. And you may find a few weaknesses to work on too.

Defining you personal brand

Use the questionnaire to think about your personal brand, to identify both strengths and weaknesses. You could also copy the questionnaire before you fill it in and give it to colleagues, superiors or friends to complete. Then compare your answers with theirs to help you develop a personal action plan.

Personal brand for (name):

- What expertise do I offer my team?

- What results do I guarantee management?

- What levels of service do I offer to my customers?

- What vision do I have for my staff?

- What are my biggest strengths?

- What are my most important weaknesses?

- Which personal trait of mine is most valued by others?

- What skills do I have that others do not?

- My brand statement (maximum 20 words):

- What should I do next to develop and promote my personal brand?

What do you say?

The 'pull style' of influencing

Introduce your view
- *Can I start? As I see it, …*
- *Shall we start with you? What do you think about this?*

Listen to the views of others
- *So for you, the important thing is …*
- *Why do you …?*

Encourage compromise
- *How far would / could you …?*
- *Would you be willing to …?*

Agree on a win-win solution
- *So, can we agree that …?*
- *Would that be a good solution for you?*

The 'push style' of influencing

Explain the situation
- *First, let's look at the facts.*
- *We need to accept the fact that …*

Introduce your own convincing proposals
- *It is my strong belief that …*
- *The facts clearly show that …*

Deal with objections strongly
- *Actually, that's wrong because …*
- *That argument is not really correct.*

Push agreement towards your proposals
- *So, I think we can agree to …*
- *I think we're in a position to decide that …*

Techniques for influencing people

Stress the benefits
- *The main benefit for you would be …*
- *This would enable you to …*

Build trust
- *In my experience we should …*
- *This worked very well in my last project.*

Be transparent
- *I've divided my explanation into two sections.*
- *My reason for saying this is …*

Use logical arguments
- *The main reason behind my argument is …*
- *The figures show that …*

Focus on the relationship
- *I understand your feelings.*
- *You know me well, so …*

Be strong (and confident)
- *There is no other solution.*
- *I have no doubt that …*
- *I am very confident that …*

Look to the future
- *My vision is …*
- *I'd like to tell you a story.*

Show optimism
- *I'm very optimistic about this, because …*
- *The best case scenario is that we can …*

Dealing with 'no'

Type of objection	What is said	How to respond
Morality	*That isn't ethical.*	Disagree: *Actually, I think it is fair and honest to …*
Analysis	*We need more data.*	Make concrete: *Which data do you need exactly?*
Experience	*We've tried this before.*	Focus on now: *Yes, but the current situation is different.*
Priorities	*I have something else to do.*	Stress risks: *OK, but if we don't make a decision on this, then …*
Fear of failure	*What if this goes wrong?*	Show understanding: *I agree that we need to be careful so …*
Ignorance	*I don't understand.*	Be patient: *Let me go over it again.*
Power play	*I cannot agree to this.*	Escalate: *Fine, but then I will need to go back to my manager …*
Fear of change	*I think many people will react negatively to the change.*	Explain opportunities: *I know, but I think we can take this opportunity to …*

8 DEALING WITH 'DIFFICULT PEOPLE'

> **Eventually we will find (mostly in retrospect, of course) that we can be very grateful to those people who have made life most difficult for us.**
>
> Ayya Khema, German-born Buddhist nun (1923–97)

When communication breaks down and misunderstanding or conflict arises, we can be quick to label others as the reason for the problem: he doesn't listen, or she isn't open. We tend to think that the problem is caused by 'difficult people'. However, we may be looking at the problem in the wrong way. The difficulty may not be in others but more in ourselves.

In this unit we look at how to manage people who we see as difficult and how to manage our views on these people. We look at how to avoid communication breakdowns, and how to deal with them when they do happen.

Before you read on, think about these questions:

1 Why do we see others as difficult?

2 How can we communicate with others more openly?

3 How can we manage our impatience?

4 What are the advantages of working more closely with people we find difficult?

Towards more open communication

1 Why do we see others as difficult and what can we do about it?

Dealing with our own prejudices is difficult. We each build a picture of the world that makes sense to us and helps us to live our lives. When someone else challenges this mental model, for example, by wearing different clothes, having a different sense of humour, disagreeing in a meeting, or organising a project in a different way, we often have a very basic reaction: to defend ourselves and attack the behaviour of the other.

This behaviour can be difficult to control but, to become effective communicators, we need to recognise this basic reflex and to learn to manage it. We need to learn to be more open when others challenge us, and to see these moments of 'difference' as learning opportunities.

2 Three steps to more open communication

How can we learn to communicate with others more openly? First, we need to accept that nobody has a monopoly on the truth. There are many different ways of making sense of a complex world, so rather than defending our own view, we should start by consciously and regularly challenging our own ideas and opinions, particularly in situations when we become emotional and make negative judgements about other people.

Openness is especially important when working in multicultural environments, because people's values and behaviours can be so different. If we become irritated or frustrated by those who do not do things our way, our communication is affected and we limit the ability to work together effectively.

The solution is to think more about *how* we think, and to select positive rather than negative communication behaviours. The three steps in this process are to:

1 recognise our negative interpretations of someone else's behaviour
2 analyse the possible meanings of the behaviour fairly in order to develop a more positive understanding
3 adopt a positive communication strategy to deal with the behaviour based on this more positive analysis.

The table gives three cases of this three-stage process.

	Stage 1 Recognising negative interpretation	Stage 2 Analysing another's behaviour fairly	Stage 3 Choosing a positive communication strategy
Case 1	'This person is very arrogant. He loves the sound of his own voice. He talks far too much and dominates most of the meetings he is in. He doesn't listen and never asks other people what they think. He's really difficult to work with.'	'This person may be justifiably confident in his own expertise and thus believes he has the answers to most problems. It's possible that he sees his contributions as wholly constructive. He may believe that a good professional gives long and complete inputs in discussions. He may not have the necessary skills to summarise complex arguments in a simple way. He may ask few questions because he expects others to provide input if they have something they want to say, rather than to wait to be asked.'	'It could be useful to discuss ground rules for meetings to avoid domination by certain speakers. It could also be useful to find a polite and constructive way of interrupting this person. I may need in the short term to accept his communication style although I'll try and show him that it's not always appreciated or helpful and that we may both need to adapt to the style of the other in order to communicate successfully.'
Case 2	'She's a poor leader. She doesn't know the jobs of the people she's managing. She never gives clear direction and she just expects others to solve problems on their own. She's weak. In meetings, she just listens and lets discussions go on and on.'	'This may be a case of uncertain leadership. It could be that she has a poor grasp of the management demands of her position and so doesn't provide clear direction. It could also be that she sees leadership more in terms of empowerment than directing. She may trust her employees to do their jobs properly and may want to encourage personal confidence and responsibility rather than dependence. Her listening style could be an expression of this.'	'One strategy could be to discuss the expectations that this manager has of her staff. If done in a constructive way, this could lead to better working practice. If she demands a different type of response from her team from the one they are giving, greater flexibility from team members may be necessary. If her behaviour is due to weaknesses in management knowledge or leadership skills, then the situation should be handled sensitively, although training and coaching may help.'

	Stage 1 Recognising negative interpretation	Stage 2 Analysing another's behaviour fairly	Stage 3 Choosing a positive communication strategy
Case 3	'She always seems to argue and become aggressive and competitive in discussions. She tends to criticise others and never sees that she may be partly responsible. She can never admit that she has made a mistake.'	'This could be someone who sees herself as having strong views on a subject on which she's an expert (which may be fully justified). She may also be able to separate the topic from the person in discussions. So while she may appear aggressive, she's not being personal but simply interrogating the topic. It's also possible that her criticism of others hides insecurity about herself, which could need careful handling.'	'It's important to remain emotionally calm during discussions with combative individuals. Remember, such people can't make you angry themselves; anger is created by you losing emotional control. So I need to manage my emotions. If necessary, I can try and communicate to her in private the effect her behaviour is having on others. She may be unaware of the negative feelings she's generating and be open to change. It could also be helpful to clarify with her some ground rules for effective communication.'

Managing impatience

The ability to move from interpretation (stage 2) to a more positive analysis and an effective communication strategy (stage 3) requires a lot of effort and emotional control. This is especially difficult for people who are under time pressure, because impatience often destroys opportunities to think in a more constructive way.

Although we sometimes connect impatience with positive values – our own efficiency or our ability to see the correct solution faster than others – it is actually a signal of our intolerance. Impatience can destroy relationships by sending messages of disrespect and distrust. This means it has to be managed as a matter of priority. Take the test on page 88 to find out how impatient you are.

Now let us look at how to manage impatience. There are two main steps in this process:

1 Know the causes

Start paying attention to what starts off your feelings of impatience. Is it how someone talks in a meeting? Is it a particular style of email? Are you more likely to be impatient in the morning or later in the day? Keep a diary of your reactions and look for patterns. Ask people who know you to describe how you look and what you say when you are impatient. This will help you to recognise and to control the emotion.

2 Learn self-control

Here are some thoughts and questions to help you to control your impatience:

1 Recognise that impatience can destroy effective communication. Do you want to be ineffective?

2 Remember that the only person who can make you feel impatient is you. The final responsibility for feeling impatient does not lie with anyone else, only with you.

3 If you start to feel impatient, 'step outside' the emotion as it rises inside you. Imagine watching yourself from a distance or putting the emotion in a box. At the same time, create a sense of calm by filling your mind with pleasant thoughts and memories. Try to control your breathing and posture. Re-engage with the other person and try to discover what is interesting or of value in what they are saying or doing.

4 Impatience is often generated when we feel that our agenda is not being followed or people are not listening to us. So forget your agenda and invest more time in understanding the other person's point of view. In discussion, avoid at all costs saying, *Yes, but ...;* instead say *Why do you say that?*

As you begin to think more and engage with the other person, your negative feelings will decrease and you can try for more constructive dialogue.

3 TUF

Use the TUF approach – Time out, Understand, Framework – with people whom you find difficult. TUF is both *reflective* – asking you to analyse your own view of a situation – and *active* – suggesting things you might say or do at specific moments.

1 Time out

Take a time out and reflect on why you think someone is difficult. Ask yourself:
- What is this person actually doing that I find difficult?
- Why do I find this behaviour difficult?
- How would other people define this same behaviour?
- How would the person explain his or her own behaviour?
- What aspects of this person's behaviour may I be misinterpreting?
- What am I doing that makes the situation worse?
- What can I do to improve the situation?

2 Understand

The second step is to check your understanding of the motivation and meaning behind the other person's message.

3 Framework

The third step is to set a framework for effective dialogue. See the *What do you say?* section for ideas about how to deal with different kinds of 'difficult person'.

Moving forward

Few of us get the chance to choose our colleagues and business partners, so there will always be people whom we find frustrating and situations that we find difficult. If we want more effective workplace relationships, the real challenge is to manage our basic human tendency to classify particular people and reactions as difficult.

Taking time to understand ourselves – our reactions, prejudices and fears – is a good starting point, although this can also be quite painful. We have to admit weakness and start learning from those who can really challenge us. If we can commit to this approach, we have an opportunity to reduce the potential for conflict and its impact in the workplace. And we can produce a communication culture in which diversity produces real benefits for ourselves, others and our organisation.

What do you say?

Checking your understanding

Questions to understand motivation
- *That's interesting. Why do you think this?*
- *This sounds important. Could you tell me more about your thinking?*

Questions to clarify language
- *What do you mean by 'expensive'?*
- *Why do you say 'difficult'?*

Questions to develop the conversation
- *So what will happen if …?*
- *So when would you want to …?*
- *So who do you think should …?*

Setting a framework for dominators

Check other opinions
- *Mr Hu, this is important. Can we hear what others think about your idea?*

Follow an agreed rule
- *Jan, sorry to interrupt you, but we agreed to hear everybody's view. OK?*

Express feelings
- *Paulo, I'm a little frustrated here, since I feel I don't have a chance to say anything.*

Setting a framework for arguers

Challenge
- *Jackie, you seem to be against this. What's your proposal?*

Appeal to the arguer's team spirit
- *Helen, this is not a competition. Let's try to be as constructive as possible.*

Stop negativity
- *I feel your inputs are a little negative, Christophe. What, for you, would be a positive way forward?*

Setting a framework for shy people

Involve the person personally
- *Zhao Li, what's your view?*

Go to a breakout
- *Let's break out into smaller groups and discuss the problem and then come together in fifteen minutes to share ideas. Jo, would you join my group?*

Prepare in advance
- *OK, let me try to summarise everyone's views, which I collected in advance. Fatima thinks ...*

Setting a framework for complainers

Accept and move on
- *Matt, I can hear that you're not happy with this, but let's try to find a solution.*

Reject blaming
- *Helga, I don't think we should blame others. That isn't fair if the other person is not here.*

Focus responsibility
- *I think we should take responsibility for this situation and find a solution.*

Setting a framework for talkers

Be clear about deadlines
- *Rashid, sorry to interrupt you, but I must write this email now.*

Postpone
- *Do you think we could discuss this in detail later?*

9 MANAGING CONFLICT

> **A good manager doesn't try to eliminate conflict, (s)he tries to keep it from wasting the energies of his (or her) people. If you're the boss and your people fight you openly when they think that you are wrong – that's healthy.**
>
> Robert Townsend, American business executive and author (1920–98)

The risks of conflict are clear. Conflict can damage relationships, reduce the motivation and creativity of individuals and teams, and lead to higher costs and lower productivity.

However, conflict also has benefits. Disagreements between individuals can be a useful way of identifying organisational problems that need to be dealt with. Conflict in diverse teams can help to avoid the problem of 'group think', when everyone thinks in the same way. And if conflict is managed successfully, people can achieve better levels of understanding, leading to better relationships and improved results.

Before you read on, think about these questions:

Q
1 What does conflict mean to you?

2 What are the main causes of conflict?

3 Why does conflict arise in teams?

4 How can you deal with conflict?

What is conflict?

The term 'conflict' is used in a wide range of contexts and with different meanings. In politics, we talk about international conflicts caused by clashes of religious values, identities and historical perspectives. At the other end of the scale, a minor disagreement in a meeting can be called a conflict of opinion. There are also conflicts of interest in business, when there is an important difference between someone's individual interests and the interests or values of their organisation.

In order to better understand conflict, think about the differences between conflict, misunderstanding and disagreement.

Conflict and misunderstanding

Conflict begins when people have opposing interests – when one person stops another from reaching a goal. In organisations, there can be conflict about anything, from booking a meeting room to major disputes over company strategy. But a misunderstanding is not necessarily a conflict. When you deal with a misunderstanding, you may find that you and the other person actually have shared interests. This is why understanding how others see a situation is so important during conflict resolution: there may be enough common interests to solve the problem quickly.

Conflict and disagreement

Conflict involves emotions: it can make people feel irritated, frustrated, angry or upset. Disagreements, on the other hand, do not necessarily involve emotions. They can be quite cool and rational: disagreements are simply differences of opinion. In conflict, it is often people's emotions that are the real challenge because they radically reduce our ability to act rationally and constructively.

Remember: Understanding and managing one's own feelings are critical to dealing with conflict successfully.

Causes of conflict

There are a number of causes of conflict. These often happen together to make the conflict more complex and more difficult to resolve. Two key causes of conflict at work are organisational change, and a lack of understanding of team dynamics.

1 Organisational change

Globalisation is causing dramatic changes to the way companies work. One example is the standardisation and centralisation or outsourcing of functions like IT and finance. These processes can increase the tensions that already exist between people working in the head office, who may struggle to maintain their authority, and people in subsidiaries, who may struggle to maintain their autonomy.

The global pressure to be competitive produces frequent restructuring, with employees facing big and often unwelcome changes to the way they work and to their responsibilities. They may need to work on change projects on top of their normal line responsibilities. And this means an increased workload, which is a further source of stress and conflict.

Managers who lead change internationally need to find the time to meet people face to face in different countries. They need to provide a clear and engaging vision that supports employees through difficult change processes, which may be far from transparent or logical. Unfortunately, leaders often communicate poorly in such situations, and they make two main mistakes:

Insufficient communication

People working internationally often do not communicate enough with their colleagues: this can create big problems in international projects. For example, what do you do if you find out halfway through a project that someone is not competent or cannot finish the job because of local requirements? Good international operators avoid these conflicts by getting to know their colleagues and their local contexts better, and by checking frequently whether agreed actions are achievable.

Insensitive communication

Working internationally demands new sensitivities. We have to recognise that communicating in our usual way – which we may consider natural, honest and open – may be a source of conflict. Our communication style may be confusing or offensive to others. For example, communicators who place a high value on directness, objectivity and what they see as an honest search for the truth, may be seen as rude, aggressive or uncultivated in cultures with a preference for more indirect communication. Likewise, indirect communicators may be seen as lacking focus or as evasive by more direct communicators.

Remember: Clear speaking, effective listening and giving useful feedback all help to build mutual understanding and to reduce the chances of conflict.

2 Team dynamics

Another common source of conflict is a lack of understanding of how teams work. Understanding the dynamics of teams involves understanding team processes and team roles. Americans Bruce W. Tuckman and Mary Ann Jensen believe that teams go through a number of stages of development, one of which – the 'storming phase' – involves conflict.

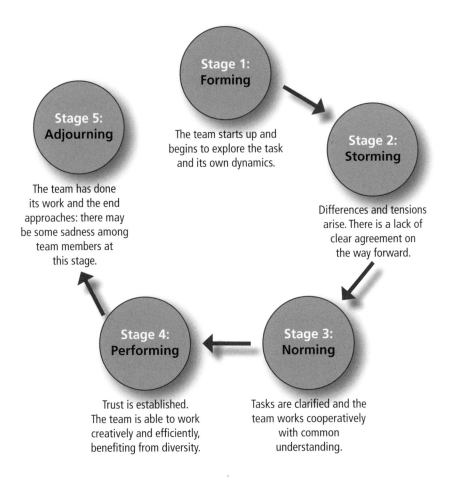

Stage 1: Forming

The team starts up and begins to explore the task and its own dynamics.

Stage 2: Storming

Differences and tensions arise. There is a lack of clear agreement on the way forward.

Stage 3: Norming

Tasks are clarified and the team works cooperatively with common understanding.

Stage 4: Performing

Trust is established. The team is able to work creatively and efficiently, benefiting from diversity.

Stage 5: Adjourning

The team has done its work and the end approaches: there may be some sadness among team members at this stage.

If we understand that the life of a team often develops in this way and that storming is an inevitable and even necessary phase of team development, then conflict will seem less threatening and more of a natural process that can be managed by techniques such as:

- sensitising the team to the storming phase
- stressing the value of diversity
- establishing rules early to manage conflict.

Managing diversity is critical to the good functioning of international teams. A number of psychometric models claim that teams can benefit from the right mix of different types of people doing different tasks. Knowing our own work and communication styles, and those of our colleagues, can help us to appreciate others and to adapt our behaviour to a style more appreciated by others.

Remember: More and more international leaders believe that profiling team members, using a psychometric tool like Myers Briggs or TMS (see page 96) when the team first forms, is an effective way to support mutual understanding and to avoid or help to resolve conflicts.

3 Who am I? Who are you?

The Team Management System, developed by Team Management Systems International Ltd, identifies eight common types of working style based on people's preferences in relation to the way they relate to others, the way they organise themselves and others, the way they process information, and the way they make decisions. TMS calls one of the types *Thruster-Organisers*. These are people who:
- like to organise and implement
- are quick to decide and are result-oriented
- set up systems
- are analytical
- make things happen
- take action by giving deadlines
- can put pressure on others
- may overlook people's feelings.

More managers fall into this category than any other. And, although such people may bring a sense of dynamism and focus to teamwork, they can irritate team members who like more time to reflect. To such colleagues, the *Thruster-Organiser* may appear to be pushy and impatient. So to avoid conflict within teams, *Thruster-Organisers* who understand team dynamics, try to adapt their communication style, for example, by speaking more slowly, giving others more time to express their views, and stating clearly that these views are valued.

Ask yourself: Are you a *Thruster-Organiser?* What could you change to make it easier for others to work with you?

4 Culture and personality

Cultural difference is another cause of conflict which is often put forward. Much has been written about how different attitudes to, for example, time, hierarchy or structure may lead to conflict. In fact, our attitudes towards these dimensions may be due to our personalities as much as to our cultural backgrounds. But they can still cause difficulties. Sometimes it can be little things like the tone of someone's voice or someone's sense of humour that creates tensions between people. In such situations, we need to remember two things. First, as Stephen R. Covey, the management guru, says, 'Strength lies in differences, not similarities'. Second, we should try to understand that being irritated by other people is not the result of their failing but of ours. Irritation, impatience and anger towards others usually say more about the limits of our own tolerance than about the qualities of others.

Remember: One of the most important skills in diversity management is being able to interact positively with people whom you may not feel very positively about.

Dealing with conflict

There are many ways of dealing with conflict. The approach you use will depend on the specific people and situation. And you need to choose your strategy carefully. For example, if you do not have the necessary authority, you may not even have the right to challenge another person. Five possible strategies for dealing with conflict are shown in this diagram:

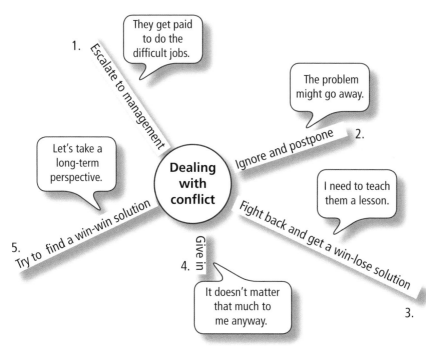

The win-win approach to conflict conversations

The choice of format for dealing with conflict is also wide, ranging from an informal one-to-one meeting over coffee to a more formal mediation or arbitration process involving external parties. Here we look at how you might handle a fairly formal meeting with members of your department or team.

Preparing for the meeting

You need to do some preparatory work to ensure that a resolution is reached in the face-to-face discussion. You should:

- Establish the facts of the case, including claims and counter-claims.
- Understand any legal issues involved.
- Research the feelings and needs of the participants.
- Set clear goals for the meeting in advance in writing.
- Plan what to say if people get emotional.

Starting the meeting

It is important to create a professional and positive atmosphere quickly. You also need to establish clearly the purpose and the process of the discussion. So:
- Open positively.
- Express your hope that a solution can be found.
- State clearly the need to show respect for others.
- Clarify the agenda and timetable.
- Negotiate a process.
- Should you present your views first or let others speak? Talking first can be helpful to stop others using negative arguments at the start. On the other hand, showing empathy by listening first may bring a resolution faster.

Managing the meeting

Emotions can run high when discussing a conflict. This makes it difficult to keep people thinking constructively. Here are some ideas to keep the dialogue solution-oriented:
- Keep the atmosphere positive.
- Leave more difficult items until later.
- Be polite.
- Let people give their views.
- Acknowledge other people's feelings.
- Minimise loss of face for all.
- Give positive feedback.

All this is easier said than done when dealing with people who may be very emotional. Check the tips for handling 'difficult' communicators in Unit 8.

Closing the meeting

At the end of the meeting, summarise any agreement and finish on the right note, looking forward and not back:
- Summarise the agreement and clarify responsibilities for the next steps.
- Set a timetable for reviewing the next steps to ensure that they are implemented.
- Take time to celebrate success and re-affirm working relationships.

Self-assessment

The final phase of the meeting happens when it is over. Take a few minutes to write down what you thought went well and what you might do differently in the future. Use these questions to help you. This kind of exercise can help you to improve your performance next time.

Build, don't destroy

Conflict brings with it some opportunities and many risks. If we allow ourselves to become over-emotional in conflict situations, we may put our professional reputation and career at risk. Damaging relationships now may limit our ability to deliver results in the future. So focus your energies on building good relationships and dealing with any conflicts that may arise when they arise.

Managing meetings: Feedback

Answer these questions to give yourself feedback on your ability to manage conflict in meetings.

How well did I do on the following points?
Rate yourself from 1 (the lowest mark) to 6 (the highest mark).

	Low					High
	1	2	3	4	5	6
Was I prepared?	○	○	○	○	○	○
Was I clear?	○	○	○	○	○	○
Was I flexible?	○	○	○	○	○	○
Was I creative?	○	○	○	○	○	○
Was I positive?	○	○	○	○	○	○
Was I determined?	○	○	○	○	○	○
Was I persuasive?	○	○	○	○	○	○
Was I fair?	○	○	○	○	○	○
Was I successful?	○	○	○	○	○	○

What will I do differently next time?

Total [ ]

Photocopy this feedback form so that you can use it more than once.

What do you say?

Stages of team development: The storming phase

Sensitising the team to the storming phase
- *We may meet problems as we try to find a way of working together.*

Stressing the value of diversity
- *Our different working styles will help us to be more innovative.*

Establishing rules early to manage conflict
- *If there is a conflict, let's agree to solve it by …*

Starting a conflict resolution meeting

Open positively by expressing optimism
- *I appreciate that people have very different views, but I'm confident that we can find a solution today.*
- *Let's see if we can find a consensus on how to proceed.*

State clearly the need for respect
- *I think it's important that we keep a positive atmosphere in this meeting.*
- *Let's try to show respect for each other in the meeting.*

Clarify the agenda and timetable
- *I suggest we discuss the issues in the order that they appear on the agenda. Is everyone happy with that?*
- *Does anyone have any comments on the agenda or shall we move on to the first point?*

Present your views (or invite others to present theirs)
- *I'd like to start by saying how I see this question. Is that OK?*
- *I'd like to start by hearing more about how you see the issue.*

Managing a conflict resolution meeting

Keep your tone positive
- *I'm confident we can find a solution.*

Be fair to others
- *That's a good point.*

Leave difficult items until later
- *Maybe we should come back to this later.*

Be polite
- *I'm not sure that is really the case.*

Encourage others
- *Please go on.*

Manage negativity in others
- *Can we try to keep things as positive as possible?*

Acknowledge feelings
- *I appreciate how you feel.*

Give positive feedback
- *I think you've been doing a great job.*

Encourage creative thinking
- *Is there another way to look at this?*

Explore possibilities
- *If I did this, would you …?*

Sell your solution
- *I think the real benefit of this is …*

Exert pressure
- *I think we need to be realistic about this.*

Managing difficult moments in conflict resolution meetings

Difficult moment	Possible responses	
Someone rejects your agenda *This isn't the main issue.*	**Assert your feelings** *But it's an important issue for me.*	**Ask questions and listen** *What is the main issue for you?*
Someone puts on pressure by using 'must' *We must do this. There's no choice.*	**Ask them to explain** *Why do you reject the other options?*	**Reject the word 'must'** *I don't like the use of 'must'.*
Someone predicts disaster *If we don't do this, the project will fail.*	**Stress other options** *I do think there are other options.*	**Reject the forecast** *That's an overstatement, I think.*
Someone externalises *I can't do that. Customers will refuse.*	**Question the tactic** *Which customers have you spoken to?*	**Contradict** *But customers do want this.*
Someone quotes the rules *This is what it says in the guidelines.*	**Appeal to creativity** *Let's think creatively for a moment.*	**Correct the analysis** *In fact, the rules say that …*
Someone focuses on their own data *How can you disagree with these figures?*	**Put the facts into context** *This only shows part of the picture.*	**Focus on feelings** *We must think about people too.*
Someone adds time pressure *I need an answer today.*	**Stress the importance of quality** *We need a lasting solution.*	**Say you need time** *I really need to think this over.*

Difficult moment	Possible responses	
Someone gets personal *You don't trust me.*	**Question the tactic** *Let's try not to make this personal.*	**Focus on feelings** *Why do you feel that way?*
Someone generalises *You never inform me about anything.*	**Focus on specifics** *Let's concentrate on this case, please.*	**Question the strategy** *Generalisations aren't helpful.*
Someone threatens you *I'll have to go over your head on this one.*	**Remain open** *OK, if you feel that's your only option.*	**Question the tactic** *Is that really a good idea?*

Closing the conflict resolution meeting

Summarise and clarify responsibilities for the next steps
- *Let me just summarise what we've agreed on today.*
- *I'd like to clarify the next steps for each of us.*

Define a timetable to review the next steps
- *Should we agree on a schedule to review progress?*
- *I think it's very important to define a schedule to check on progress. Do you agree?*

Take time to celebrate success and reaffirm working relationships
- *I think we've done a good job. Well done.*
- *That was a tough meeting, but I think it has been a very positive discussion.*
- *I think we've started to work well together now and I hope that we can keep this up in the future.*

10 GIVING AND GETTING FEEDBACK

"
Feedback is the breakfast of champions.

Ken Blanchard, American author and management guru (1939–)
"

Feedback is everywhere in business. Companies ask customers if they are pleased with their services. Participants fill out evaluation forms ('happy sheets') after training courses. Managers and staff take part in appraisal interviews. Colleagues give each other informal feedback during conversations round the coffee machine.

The goal of feedback is simple: to improve performance. Feedback can help individuals and organisations to learn from the past and to develop competitive advantages in the future. Feedback helps people to think about their strengths and to identify areas to work on. Feedback can be central to the success of an organisation.

In this unit we look in particular at some of the key aspects of more formal manager-report feedback, although many of the ideas can also be applied to more informal everyday feedback conversations. Before you read on, think about these questions:

1 Why do we give feedback?

2 How is feedback influenced by culture and by personality?

3 What are the key skills for giving feedback?

4 What are the key skills for receiving feedback?

Why do we give feedback?

Feedback has three main objectives:

1 The objective of developmental feedback (also called 'constructive feedback') is to help people to develop and to become more effective. It is a basic responsibility of any manager to give this kind of feedback. It means looking at performance and skills levels, and providing constructive guidance to individuals and groups on how to improve. Without such feedback, employees will probably fail to develop as fast and as far as they can.

2 Affirmative feedback simply means telling people that they did a good job. This explicit praising can satisfy an emotional need for recognition, and boost motivation and performance. Without praise, many employees become frustrated and demotivated.

3 With motivated employees who are developing skills and realising their potential, both kinds of feedback also help organisations to work better.

Feedback and culture

Culture relates to feedback in two main ways. First, feedback styles are influenced by culture. Second, it is the responsibility of leaders to create a 'feedback culture' in their teams, departments or organisations.

1 Being sensitive to culture

Certain styles of feedback tend to be associated with certain national or organisational cultures. For example, a more direct form of feedback is often preferred in northern European business cultures, whereas in other parts of the world an indirect style reflects a preference for harmony.

Attitudes to risk and quality may also influence the style of feedback in an organisation. Some organisations suffer from a 'blame culture' in which mistakes are not tolerated and strong criticism is voiced. This kind of environment makes openness and constructive feedback more difficult.

In very hierarchical organisations, feedback often only goes in one direction, namely from the top down. In collectivist or group-oriented environments, praising one individual may not be appropriate, and feedback is usually delivered to the whole team.

There are no rights or wrongs in this area. Direct feedback may sometimes work more effectively than softer and more polite indirect feedback – it all depends on the context. Managers need to be culturally sensitive and flexible.

Ask yourself: How effectively can and do you adapt your feedback style to different cultural contexts? If you work internationally, ask someone with a different cultural background from you to give you informal feedback on the way different people see your style.

2 Creating a feedback culture

People working in international teams and organisations need to create a common understanding about how they are going to work together. One way to do this is to discuss expectations and define team rules. For example:

- No interrupting people during meetings.
- Acknowledge emails within 24 hours, and deal with them within three working days.
- No escalation of problems to local management without internal team discussion first.

During this 'forming' process, team leaders and members can establish a culture in which constructive feedback is frequently asked for and openly given. Feedback is particularly important as a way of dealing with misunderstandings among people with different values, expectations and behaviours. Team leaders should model the style of feedback they wish to create, and should discuss this with their project deputies. These sub-project heads will then feel more confident about giving feedback to their team members, who may also be inspired to give peer-to-peer feedback.

In this way a feedback culture begins to develop. But to maintain the feedback culture, team leaders need to make sure that team members know how to give and to listen to feedback. This may require training at an early stage in the team's formation.

To help you to create a positive feedback culture, think about these questions:

Why? What are the objectives of feedback here? Are there any areas in which feedback will be especially useful?

How often? Is feedback to be given only once a year at a formal appraisal interview, or will it be an informal, daily process?

Who? Who should give feedback? Is it a top-down process only, or can it also be bottom-up, with employees giving feedback to their managers? Is peer-to-peer feedback encouraged?

How? Does everyone have the same expectations? Do those receiving feedback just want some praise, or are they interested in learning how to improve? What style of feedback will be most effective with each member of the team?

Where? Is feedback to be given individually and privately, or openly, for example, in team meetings? Is information exchanged during feedback confidential, or can it be communicated to others in the organisation?

Ask yourself: How can you help to create a feedback culture within the group that you work in?

3 Personality and feedback

National and organisational factors influence how feedback is given and received, but personality has a big impact too. People vary enormously in how open they are to receiving feedback, and in their capacity for personal change. You must think about this before you decide on both the content and the style of the feedback which you want to give someone. Sensitive managers tune into the people in front of them, and use different feedback styles in different situations.

Ask yourself: How far do you fine-tune your feedback style to suit different individual personalities?

How to give feedback

Giving and receiving feedback are key responsibilities and key skills for every leader. Here are 11 tips to help you:

1 Get the timing right

Feedback is best given as soon as possible after a particular event (although let the person receiving the feedback share in deciding the best time and place). Make sure that there is enough time to talk things through: different opinions may make the discussion longer.

2 Structure the meeting

Ideally, feedback is asked for rather than imposed, so if you are giving feedback to a direct report, you need to manage the process with special care. It is essential to be clear about your general intention, for example, *I'd like to give you a little feedback about ...*, and about the positive motivation behind your feedback, for example, *I think this can help you to ....* This helps to ensure that employees remain open to the opportunity for development.

3 Start by listening

Encourage employees to assess themselves so that you can build on their own personal insights. People are often more willing to accept developmental feedback when they recognise their own strengths and weaknesses. In this phase it is important to listen. Do not give your own opinion too soon, but instead ask questions to encourage reflection and discussion. Rather than saying *I don't think anyone was very happy with the way you led the meeting*, you could ask *How did you feel about the meeting? How do you think other people felt about it?*

4 Comment, don't evaluate

One key feedback skill is to comment neutrally on the behaviour you have observed, rather than to offer (negative) interpretations or judgements. For example, saying *Your first input to the meeting took ten minutes* is more likely to encourage discussion than saying *You dominated the meeting*. Focus on specific facts and encourage employees to make their own assessments.

5 Talk about impact

Encourage employees to think about their impact on other people, for example, by asking a question like *If you make a presentation in this way in front of clients, do you think there is a danger that ...?* Often the impact of our behaviour is not what we intended, so we need to become aware of the impact that our behaviour could have, and to think about alternatives.

6 Look at perception gaps

It is very helpful to contrast the way we see ourselves with the way others see us. But we need to choose our language carefully so that we do not give people negative labels. For example, do not say *You are very dominant and people don't like that,* but rather *You may see yourself as a strong person. Others might see this behaviour as rather aggressive.* The use of 'may' and 'might' encourages people to see themselves through the eyes of others.

7 Explore alternatives

Help individuals to reflect on what they could do differently. During this phase, give people time to reflect on your feedback and to consider another way of doing things. Allow for periods of silence during this phase and treat these as positive: it means that the person you are giving feedback to is thinking about what you are saying!

8 Offer realistic suggestions

Sometimes you will need to suggest alternatives but try to build on suggestions which come from the employee. Be specific about how the individual can improve. Stress that the objective is to change behaviour, not personality. Make people aware that behavioural change takes time and needs commitment.

9 Be sensitive to resistance

Individuals can feel threatened by feedback. People with low self-esteem tend to hear only the negative messages. People with high self-esteem may hear only the positive messages. So observe and listen carefully to check that the feedback has been received as you intended.

10 Summarise and agree on a plan

If you are giving feedback to a report, summarise the objective and outcome of the feedback clearly, in order to get commitment to measurable actions. Agree on a process to track progress and make sure the plan is implemented. End on an optimistic note to motivate the person further.

11 Get feedback on your feedback

Ask people what they valued about the conversation so that you can improve your skills. If we offer feedback, it is important that we are open to feedback ourselves.

A four-phase process for giving feedback

Here is a model which shows four different phases for feedback:

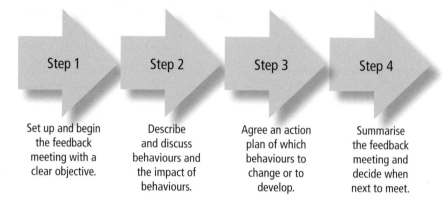

Step 1	Step 2	Step 3	Step 4
Set up and begin the feedback meeting with a clear objective.	Describe and discuss behaviours and the impact of behaviours.	Agree an action plan of which behaviours to change or to develop.	Summarise the feedback meeting and decide when next to meet.

Handling people who do not want feedback

Some people hear feedback as criticism and defend themselves by rejecting observations and blaming the situation or other people. Here are some ideas for handling these 'difficult' people:

1 Reflect on your authority to give feedback

Feedback can fail if the person giving it is not respected. For example, they may be seen as too young, too junior or the wrong gender in the eyes of the person receiving feedback. If your feedback is not working, think about how the other person may view your right to provide feedback.

2 Point out any unconstructive behaviour as it happens

If someone is interrupting, being defensive and generally not listening, it may be necessary to tell them that you feel that the way they are listening – or not listening – is not helpful.

3 Challenge people who over-simplify the solution

Some people claim to be flexible, and suggest it will be easy for them to change their behaviour. (*Sure, I'll speak more slowly at the next meeting so that people can understand. No problem.*) It may be necessary to insist on further meetings to review progress.

4 Make clear the consequences of people's behaviour

This can help to make people think again about the way they behave. For example, you could say *If you continue to talk over people during our meetings, I may have to ask you to stop talking altogether because it's making other people angry.* This gives people a simple choice: continue their behaviour and create a negative impact, or adapt and create a more constructive atmosphere.

5 Challenge people to be better team players and leaders

Highly talented and task-oriented individuals may not be very open to feedback. They are successful so why should they change? In cases like these, it may be helpful to appeal to teamwork, stressing the importance of collaboration and the need to develop the performances of others.

Giving feedback to your boss

Managers tend to get less feedback than anyone else, and some senior managers think that they are successful enough not to need any feedback. Only in flatter business cultures do leaders normally receive input from employees in upward appraisal interviews. Yet feedback to leaders can be extremely valuable for an organisation. Here are three tips:

1 Select the right strategy

Some managers are happy to hear straight talking from staff members; others need more sensitive handling. You may need to ask permission to give feedback. If giving upward feedback is not possible, you may want to involve another person who has the trust or authority to handle this conversation.

2 Focus on impact

Concentrate on the effect of the leader's behaviour on you or others, not on the intention behind the behaviour. When people feel challenged, they often start to defend themselves. Focus on specific things that were said and done, and show how they generated negative feelings among staff members.

3 Stress efficiency

Leaders may be persuaded to do things differently if they think this will improve results. Point it out if the leader's behaviour has damaged motivation and stress the tangible results that can be achieved by alternative behaviours.

How to receive feedback

Feedback helps us do better next time, but if our performance was not very good the first time, then we may not enjoy receiving feedback on a failure or a weakness. Yet to improve, we have to understand how others see us. So first, we need to think about which aspect of our performance (for example, our leadership, listening or technical skills) we would like feedback on. Then we need the courage to ask for feedback from others.

Feedback can be hard to take sometimes. It can feel like a criticism. We may even feel it is wrong, misguided or unfair. However, feedback is always useful information about how other people see us and the situation. We need to understand that opinion and be able to learn from it, and even change what we are doing if necessary. To understand feedback, we must be able to listen. Here are some ideas for improving your listening skills when you receive feedback.

- Listen patiently: Don't interrupt. Stay cool, even when there is criticism.
- Listen curiously: Don't defend yourself. Clarify the feedback with follow-up questions.
- Listen actively: Re-formulate what the person says to check that you have understood.
- Listen concretely: Ask for specific examples of your behaviour to help you understand.
- Listen positively: Give positive feedback to the speaker to encourage him or her to say more.
- Listen physically: Maintain eye contact and use the right body language to show interest in the feedback.
- Listen developmentally: Admit mistakes and ask for ideas on what you could do differently.
- Listen creatively: Discuss your own ideas for what you could do differently.
- Listen pragmatically: The objective of feedback is to change, so aim for a practical action plan.
- Listen continually: Make sure you get ongoing feedback to check if you are developing.

Listening is hard work, particularly when we hear things that we do not like. So after feedback, you can also ask for feedback on your listening skills to check how open you were.

Amazing feedback

Managers and coaches who spend a lot of time giving feedback to people working in international teams sometimes hear people say *Oh, yes. I've had this feedback before.* A good reply to this is *Fine. Try to make it the last time you hear it.*

Changing our behaviour is difficult and we often overestimate our ability to behave differently. The only way to know whether or not we have acted successfully on feedback is, of course, to get more feedback. If we keep getting the same feedback over a long period, we may find that we need a coach to help us move forward in a more structured and organised way.

But generally, getting regular feedback from our colleagues – peers, reports and managers – and customers, can be such a powerful way to improve performance that when we look back over a period of getting good feedback, we can be amazed at how far we have travelled.

Feedback self-assessment

How good do you feel you are at giving and receiving feedback? Make a list of your strengths and weaknesses, and think of suggestions for an action plan to improve your performance.

Self-assessment: Giving feedback

My strengths

My weaknesses

My action plan

Self-assessment: Receiving feedback

My strengths

My weaknesses

My action plan

What do you say?

Giving feedback

Set up a feedback meeting
- I'd like to give you some feedback about the meeting yesterday. When would be a good time for you?
- Could we do a short debrief on the meeting yesterday? I have one or two points I'd like to discuss with you.
- Would you like some feedback from me on how the meeting went yesterday? When would be a good time?

Clarify the objective
- Before we start, let me just go over the main objective of this feedback meeting.
- The objective of this feedback is to help you improve your performance.
- I think there are two things that could help to improve your performance.
- What would you like to get from this feedback session?

Start by listening
- How do you think the meeting went?
- How do you think you performed?
- Do you think you could have done anything differently?
- Can you tell me more about that? How did you feel? How do you think the others felt?

Comment, don't evaluate
- I thought some of the participants were a bit confused.
- I wasn't sure that everyone understood the purpose clearly.
- You said that you felt the project was going too slowly. Why did you say that? Was it useful to say that?

Talk about impact
- Roas got very annoyed at one point.
- Juan seemed to get rather angry when you said that Susanne should lead the project.
- What do you think the impact was on the Spanish team when you took that decision?
- How do you think Juan felt when you said that?

Look at perception gaps
- Why did you say that?
- What were you trying to achieve?
- How do you think you came across to the others?
- How do you think other people might interpret this behaviour?

Explore alternatives
- Could you have done that differently?
- Is there anything else you could have done?
- What could you do differently next time?
- What would have happened if you had ...?

Offer realistic suggestions
- *I think that next time you need to … / should think about … / should try … / could …*
- *I suggest that you give everyone the chance to express their views first.*
- *It may be useful to consider allowing more time for …*
- *One thing you could try is to …*

Check for understanding
- *What's your reaction to this?*
- *How do you feel about this feedback?*
- *What did you think about my last comment?*
- *Do you think it would be useful if you made a short summary at this point?*

Summarise and agree on a plan
- *So I suggest that next time you try to … and see if this helps to …*
- *Let me try and summarise. The objective today was to …*
- *In terms of outcomes, you have said that in future you'll …*
- *When do you think you can do this by?*

Get feedback on your feedback
- *Was that useful?*
- *How far was that a useful process for you?*
- *Can you give me some feedback on my feedback?*
- *Would you like any other feedback?*

Receiving feedback

Asking for feedback
- *How did I do?*
- *I would really value your feedback on …*
- *Could you give me some feedback on my presentation yesterday?*
- *How do you think I handled the meeting?*

Listening curiously
- *Why do you say that?*
- *What do you mean?*
- *What did I do exactly?*

Listening actively
- *So you mean that I should have involved people more in the preparations?*
- *If I understand you correctly, you think that Juan thought that I was threatening his authority.*
- *So you thought that I wasn't really familiar with the figures?*

Listening concretely
- *What did I do / say exactly?*
- *Have I done this before?*
- *How did Juan react?*

Listening positively
- *That's interesting.*
- *Thank you for the feedback.*
- *I'll think about that.*

Listening developmentally
- *What do you think I could / should have done?*
- *What would have been a better strategy?*
- *What would you have done?*

Listening creatively
- *Do you think I should try to …?*
- *Would it have helped if I had …?*
- *Should I be more assertive next time?*

Listen pragmatically
- *OK, I'll try (not) to … in future.*
- *Next time I will focus on …*
- *I will certainly try to improve my presentation skills.*

Listening continually
- *Am I getting better?*
- *How far do you think I have developed?*
- *Have you seen any progress?*
- *What else do you think I could be doing?*

11 WRITING EMAIL: THE BASICS

Men of few words are the best men.

William Shakespeare, English poet and playwright (1564–1616)

Email is one of the most important tools of business communication in the world today. *Business Spotlight* surveys over the past ten years consistently show that email is the communication channel used most frequently by non-native speakers of English at work, and yet it is also one of the most badly used – by native and non-native speakers alike.

The unique nature of emailing can cause problems. The first problem is that it is fast and disposable, and so does not encourage careful communication. But the bigger problem is connected to user attitudes and behaviour.

In this unit we look at some of the challenges of using email. We also propose solutions that take us back to the basic principles of communication presented in the first two units of this book. And in the next unit, we look at how to use email to carry out certain key management functions.

Before you read on, think about these questions:

1 What are the main differences between email and face-to-face communication?

2 How can you make sure that readers understand your emails?

3 How do you decide who to copy your emails to?

4 What is the best writing style for emails?

The challenges

In the first unit we outlined some basic principles of effective communication, using the sender-receiver model and T-I-P-S (Target, Information, Process, Style). We noted that:

- the sender's **T**arget must be right
- the **I**nformation must be clear
- the **P**rocess should be well defined, and that
- you should adapt your communication **S**tyle to get your message across to the receiver.

In this unit we focus on *Process* because email is primarily a channel, not a style of communication. It is a form of interaction with unique features that can make communication more difficult than when it takes place face-to-face. Here are some of the main challenges of email.

Is this a good time?

In face-to-face communication we can normally judge whether to communicate now or whether to wait until a better moment. This is not the case with email. You cannot control the conditions in which an email is read. If the recipients of your emails open them when they are busy or in a bad mood, your communication can have a negative impact, although you may be unaware of this for some time.

Tip If you want to communicate sensitive information, it may be wiser to send an email to set up a telephone call to discuss the issue directly.

What do you think?

In face-to-face communication we can watch the recipients of our messages as we talk. We can assess their levels of understanding and agreement, and can modify our message accordingly. With email, we have to send the message in one block, and we are unable to clarify or qualify what we write until we receive a reply. Emails are therefore often seen as a little aggressive or 'pushy' and can feel much more one-way than face-to-face communication.

Tip There are a number of simple techniques you can use to avoid seeming to be a little aggressive or 'pushy'.

- Start and end with basic courtesies: *Thanks for your email.*
- Encourage two-way communication by suggesting that your view may not be correct: *I may be wrong but I think we need a new approach. What do you think?*
- Show that you recognise that the other person is under pressure: *I appreciate that you are very busy ...*
- Be open to renegotiating a deadline: *If it's a problem to get me the information by the end of this week, please let me know.*
- Express thanks for support when asking for information: *I'm very grateful for your support with this.*

A question of style

In face-to-face communication we not only adapt the content of our communication to the listener but also the way we say things. This is not possible when writing an email to someone for the first time.

Tip It is safest to adopt a neutral professional style. Address people in a way that you think they will find respectful. You will be better able to assess the person's preferred style of email communication when they write back. Then you can adapt your own style accordingly.

What do you mean?

In face-to-face communication the person listening receives a message that is supported by non-verbal means of communication, such as body language or tone of voice. The reader of an email receives only the written words, making it more difficult to understand what is intended, particularly if the email has been written quickly and has been poorly constructed.

Tip Increase the clarity of your emails by using these techniques:

- Give the email a clear subject header, for example: *Meeting to discuss finances.*
- Avoid complex words and phrases.
- Organise key points into separate paragraphs that are either bulleted or numbered.
- Specify under each paragraph what the recipient has to do and by when.
- Inform the recipient why you need information by a certain date.
- Limit the number of different topics you deal with in a single email.

Who else needs to know?

In face-to-face communication the number of people you can communicate with is generally limited to how loudly you can shout – unless, of course, you are using a microphone with a large audience! With email there are no restrictions: it is possible to copy one email to thousands. A lot of people copy too many emails unnecessarily, which leads to email overload. On the other hand, you can cause resentment by not copying emails to those who feel they should be informed.

Tip Clarify expectations about copying emails, either directly with members of an international team, or via a mentor if you need advice on the policies and procedures in the organisation. Ask for feedback on a regular basis from recipients and non-recipients to check if you are getting it right. You can also get feedback on the style of your emails: too formal or informal? too much or too little information? too direct or indirect? and so on. You should always try to adapt your email style to your reader(s).

Did you get my email?

The speed of interaction in face-to-face communication is generally faster than with email. It may take a couple of days or even longer for the sender of an email to get a reply. If the receiver does not acknowledge an email, the sender is often left with the feeling that their message has disappeared into a black hole.

Tip Send short acknowledgements of emails when you think it is necessary (for example, because the subject matter is urgent) or when you think the other person would appreciate it.

What did you say?

In face-to-face communication, we exchange messages quickly but the words are forgotten almost as soon as they are spoken. Email is similarly fast for senders, but, because the words are in writing, they may have a stronger impact, particularly if the message is critical. We also lose control of the text – our emails can be copied to others without our permission – so it is important to write carefully and respectfully at all times. Your reputation can be damaged if a 'blame mail' is copied to others, so think carefully before you click 'Send'. If in doubt, store the email and review it the next day.

Look at the different ways below in which the same message can be constructed. The first version is very abrupt and potentially offensive.

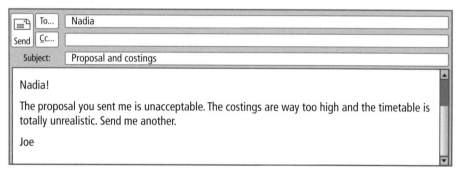

This second version is more professional and friendly.

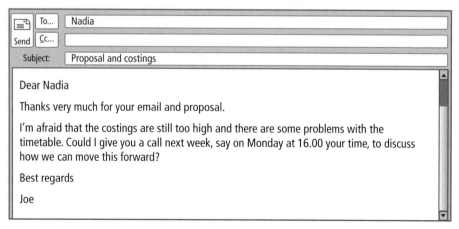

Remember, definitions of 'politeness' and 'professional' differ across cultures, so it is difficult to be sure if others will interpret your emails in a positive way. The only way to be sure is to check with international contacts and ask for feedback from time to time.

What do you write?

Writing styles

There are three major writing styles:

1 Formal: more elaborate and impersonal phrasing (legal contracts are a good example of this style).
2 Neutral professional: more direct phrases and language closer to spoken English.
3 Informal: everyday words and structures from everyday conversation.

The email style you use will depend on your reader.

Writing clear emails

Greet the reader	*Dear James*
Explain your reason for writing	*I can confirm my participation in the project meeting next week.*
State further actions	*I shall need the January sales figures to prepare my presentation. Please would you forward your results as soon as possible.*
Polite close	*Best regards*

Opening and closing

Context	Salutation	Close
Formal: you don't know the name of the recipient	*Dear Sir* *Dear Madam* *Dear Sir or Madam* *Dear Sirs* *Gentlemen* (US only)	*Yours faithfully* (UK only) *Sincerely yours* (US) *Yours truly* (US) *Sincerely* (US) *Yours sincerely* (UK)
You know the name of the recipient	*Dear Mr Smith* *Dear Mr and Mrs Smith* *Dear Ms Smith* *Dear Mrs Smith* (married) *Dear Miss Smith* (single)	*Yours sincerely*
You know someone well	*Dear John* *Hello Angela* (semi-formal) *Hi Angela* (informal)	*Best regards / Regards* *Best wishes* *Take care* (informal)
Other	*Dear all* *Hi*	*Best regards* *See you soon*

Note that:

• in British English, titles such as 'Mr' and 'Dr' are written without a full stop, but in US English, they are written with a full stop.

- email salutations for people whom you know well can be very informal and conversational, such as 'Hi', often with the person's name left out.
- 'Best regards' has almost established itself as a universal close for emails of all types, except for very informal ones.

Being sociable

Try to begin your emails positively, especially if you have to ask for something or deal with a difficult subject. A typical opening strategy is to make a polite enquiry about the person:

Hi John

How are you? How are you doing? I guess you are very busy this week …

Beginning
- *With reference to your email of 12 January, …* (formal)
- *Further to our discussion last week, …* (neutral professional)
- *How are you? Hope you are well.* (informal)

Reason for writing
- *We are writing to request …* (formal)
- *I'm just writing to confirm …* (neutral professional)
- *Just a short email to ask …* (informal)

Emailing with good news
- *We are very happy to confirm that …* (formal)
- *You will be pleased to hear that …* (neutral professional)
- *I'm happy to …* (informal)

Emailing with bad news
- *We regret to inform you that …* (formal)
- *I am afraid that … / Unfortunately, …* (neutral professional)
- *I'm sorry but …* (informal)

Requesting
- *We would appreciate it if you could …* (formal)
- *I'd be grateful if you could …* (neutral professional)
- *Could you …?* (informal)

Offering help
- *If you need more information, we would be happy to ...* (formal)
- *Would you like me to ...? / Shall I ...?* (neutral professional)
- *Do you want ...?* (informal)

Saying sorry
- *We must apologise for (not) ... / We deeply regret ...* (formal)
- *I do apologise for ... / any inconvenience caused.* (neutral professional)
- *I'm really sorry for... / about ...* (informal)

Attaching files
- *We are attaching ... / We attach ...* (formal)
- *Please find attached ...* (neutral professional)
- *I'm attaching ... / I've attached ...* (informal)

Ending
- *Do not hesitate to contact us again if you need further assistance.* (formal)
- *If you have any further questions, please contact me.* (neutral professional)
- *Let me know if you need any more help.* (informal)
- *Thanks for your help.* (informal)

Positive final comment
- *We look forward to meeting / seeing you next week.* (formal)
- *We look forward to hearing from you.* (neutral professional)
- *See you next week.* (informal)

Acronyms

ASAP	As soon as possible
BR	Best regards
BTW	By the way (informal)
FYI	For your information

Smileys
:-) = smiling face
:-(= sad face
;-) = wink

Use smileys with caution! Some people hate them.

Model emails: Make writing easy

A simple way to improve the accuracy of your emails is to use model frameworks that you can adapt with minor changes of words and facts. Take a look at the examples below and adapt them to your needs.

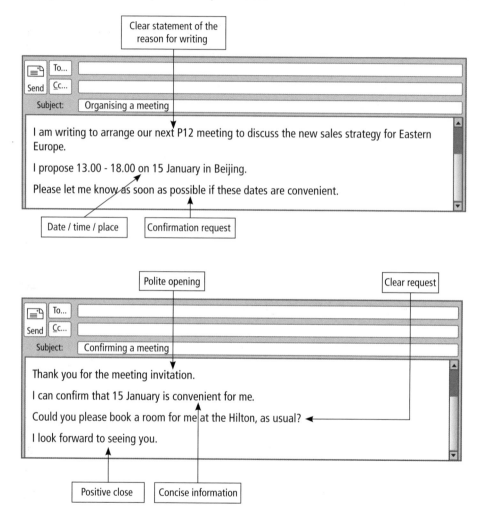

Clear statement of the reason for writing

Send | To... | Cc...

Subject: Organising a meeting

I am writing to arrange our next P12 meeting to discuss the new sales strategy for Eastern Europe.

I propose 13.00 - 18.00 on 15 January in Beijing.

Please let me know as soon as possible if these dates are convenient.

Date / time / place

Confirmation request

Polite opening

Clear request

Send | To... | Cc...

Subject: Confirming a meeting

Thank you for the meeting invitation.

I can confirm that 15 January is convenient for me.

Could you please book a room for me at the Hilton, as usual?

I look forward to seeing you.

Positive close

Concise information

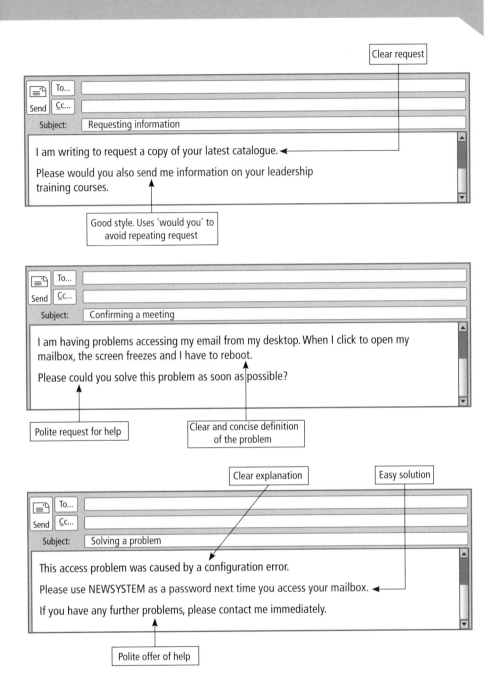

Clear request

Send | To...
Cc...
Subject: Requesting information

I am writing to request a copy of your latest catalogue.

Please would you also send me information on your leadership training courses.

Good style. Uses 'would you' to avoid repeating request

Send | To...
Cc...
Subject: Confirming a meeting

I am having problems accessing my email from my desktop. When I click to open my mailbox, the screen freezes and I have to reboot.

Please could you solve this problem as soon as possible?

Polite request for help

Clear and concise definition of the problem

Clear explanation

Easy solution

Send | To...
Cc...
Subject: Solving a problem

This access problem was caused by a configuration error.

Please use NEWSYSTEM as a password next time you access your mailbox.

If you have any further problems, please contact me immediately.

Polite offer of help

Guidelines for better emails

Here are some tips to improve your emails.

Use plain English
- *In my considered opinion ...*
- *I think that ...*

Don't repeat words unnecessarily
- *I would like to discuss sales and also to discuss a sales strategy for 2013.*
- *I would like to discuss sales and a sales strategy for 2013.*

Use a variety of sentence structures
- *Please would you send a catalogue. Please would you also confirm your 2013 prices.*
- *Please would you send a catalogue. I should be grateful if you would also confirm your 2013 prices.*

Link ideas together
- *This is an interesting suggestion. It is not possible to accept your offer.*
- *This is an interesting suggestion. However, it is not possible to accept ...*

Be consistent with contractions
- *I'd like to propose a meeting next week. I will mail you an agenda tomorrow.*
- *I'd like to propose a meeting next week. I'll mail you an agenda tomorrow.*

Simplify the date
- *We could meet on 12 January 2013.*

Be polite
- *Send me the information immediately.*
- *Could you send me the information as soon as possible?*

12 WRITING EMAIL: ADVANCED

What is written without effort is in general read without pleasure.

Samuel Johnson, English author and lexicographer (1709–84)

Section 2 of this book looked at core communication skills such as building relationships, influencing people and resolving conflicts at work in the context of face-to-face communication. However, with the rise of virtual working, it is also important to be able to manage these and other skills in the context of sending and receiving email.

Before you read on, think about these questions:

1 How can you build business relationships by email?

2 How can you influence business partners by email?

3 How can you manage conflict by email?

4 What are the dangers of using email for these communication tasks?

Building relationships

Success in business depends on building positive relationships. Email may not seem at first to be the best medium for this task: text has a more impersonal character, and it is easy to misinterpret the written word without the support of body language and tone of voice. Indeed, email can often be a source of conflict rather than harmony at work. But if we use email carefully, and in the correct combination with other media, for example with telephone and face-to-face meetings, these criticisms need not apply.

So, how can email be used to build relationships? First, we need to remember that people have different approaches to relationship-building. Some want relationships to be close and informal. They want to be friends with their colleagues, laugh with them, share more personal information, and show interest in the lives of others. *Relationship-oriented* people like this might write an email like the one below. As you read it, think about these two questions:

1 How would you feel if you received such an email?

2 How would you feel about writing such an email?

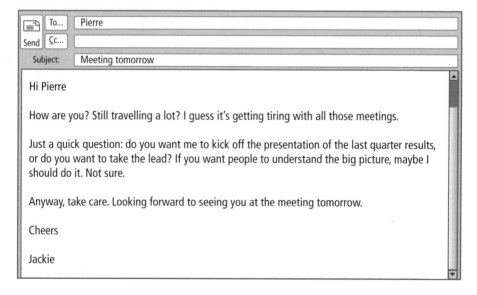

Send	To...	Pierre
	Cc...	
	Subject:	Meeting tomorrow

Hi Pierre

How are you? Still travelling a lot? I guess it's getting tiring with all those meetings.

Just a quick question: do you want me to kick off the presentation of the last quarter results, or do you want to take the lead? If you want people to understand the big picture, maybe I should do it. Not sure.

Anyway, take care. Looking forward to seeing you at the meeting tomorrow.

Cheers

Jackie

Task-oriented individuals, who often like to keep their personal and professional lives completely separate, and who often write more formally, might view this email as disrespectful and unprofessional. They might prefer to keep the tone neutral and concentrate purely on exchanging information.

The key message of this book is that communication is situational and has to be adapted to the specific person and to the specific context. If you tailor your email communication style and content to your readers, you can help to build professional respect in the same way as in face-to-face interactions.

The table below provides some tips on how you might use email to manage your relationships with two very different types of people: those who are very relationship- or affiliation-oriented, and those who very task-oriented.

Managing relationships by email

Relationship	Relationship-oriented	Task-oriented
Style	Informal Light and humorous Begin with some personal details Mention feelings Show interest in the other person	Formal Serious Focus directly on business issues and needs Stick to the facts Keep emotions out of it
Frequency	Send frequent emails to keep in touch Blend email and telephone calls	Communicate only when you need to say something Use email and avoid disturbing by phone

A task-oriented email

How would you adapt Jackie's email if you had to deliver the same message to a more task-oriented individual? Compare your answer with the model in the answer key.

Influencing people

The ability to influence others – for example, to build commitment to change or to persuade people to take on new responsibilities – is another key business skill. When you work internationally, with colleagues and customers across the world, much of this influencing has to be done by email.

As we saw in the last unit, one of the problems with emails is that we cannot choose the conditions under which they are read. The recipient may simply be in the wrong mood to be influenced positively by what you write. Nevertheless, there are some general techniques that we can use to increase our ability to influence people by email, as follows.

1 Be structured

One advantage of email is that we have the time to organise and present information logically, and to provide all the relevant detail to support an argument. In face-to-face communication, listeners can interrupt or sidetrack a speaker.

Another advantage of the written word is that the message is documented clearly. This can help as a reference point during complex negotiations or difficult discussions. Here is an example of a clearly structured email.

Send To...
Cc...
Subject:

There are three things that lead me to recommend a postponement of the project:

First, there is no budget allocated for it. This means that there are not yet enough resources available.

Second, the new global ONE-IT project is going to have an impact on every local organisation, especially in South America, so we need to wait until the effect of the project is clear.

Third, our project sponsor has just announced that she will leave the company in June. This will result in some instability, and I feel there should be a new sponsor in place before we start.

I would welcome a telephone conference as soon as possible to discuss this further.

---

2 Be interactive

Because you cannot support your email with a smile or quick clarification, it is easy for the recipient to misinterpret your motives. Use the three-step 'multimedia sandwich' to get around this problem:

Step 1

Use the telephone or a face-to-face meeting (or both) before you try to influence people in writing. Ask questions to find out their basic opinions, their key resistance points and their openness to persuasion.

Step 2

Write the email with clear arguments, and finish with a request to follow up with a telephone call or a face-to-face meeting. You may also state your willingness to consider other ideas to show openness.

Step 3

Call or meet the person(s) concerned to present your arguments, hear their responses and deal with any resistance points.

3 Use hierarchy

Another way to influence people by using email is to copy in a more senior manager. The aim here is to increase the pressure on a recipient to take your email seriously and comply with your request. However, such escalation may well be seen as an unacceptable threat, and can create negative feelings and damage a relationship, so you need to think very carefully about the different possible outcomes if you decide on this approach.

Managing conflict

Let us now look at an example of conflict management via email. The email below is from Bill Benson to Carole Schlautmann. Carole is an international project manager to whom one of Bill's line staff, Jacques Sampers, has to report as a member of her project team. Bill expresses his worries about Jacques's role in the project.

As you read the email, do the following:

1 Think about how you would feel in Carole's position.
2 Underline any parts of the email that you find problematic.
3 Think of ways that you could improve the text.

To...	Carole Schlautmann
Cc...	
Subject:	Jacques Sampers

Dear Carole

I've just got back from Manchester where I had a meeting with Jacques. As Jacques's line manager, I am becoming concerned about how much pressure you are putting him under. You know that he is seen as someone with high potential, but he seems to find working with you very demanding. I'm not sure that you understand the pressure he is under at the moment - he is managing a huge change project.

Anyway, Jacques and I had a long talk today, and he is now confident that he can deliver the results you expect, although we should talk about milestones and deadlines to really make this possible. In future, I think we should communicate more openly to avoid this kind of problem coming up again.

Regards

Bill

Bill's email could be viewed quite negatively. It seems to have an accusing tone (... *pressure you are putting him under*), and Bill seems to be saying that Carole has failed to build an effective relationship with Jacques (*I'm not sure that you understand the pressure he is under* ...). In fact, it is quite easy to identify a few techniques that Bill could use to soften his message. Here are some of the things that one might recommend:

Mix criticism in with praise ('positive framing')

Bill could have written: *Jacques really enjoys working with you and finds the project very interesting, but I am concerned about how much pressure you are putting him under.*

Be explicit about what you are *not* saying to reduce the risk of negative interpretation

Bill could have written: *I am not criticising you in any way, Carole, but I am very concerned about how much pressure Jacques is under.*

Make clear you are expressing a view, not stating facts

Bill could have written: *In my opinion, it would be a good idea to talk about milestones and deadlines* ...

These all look like good techniques, and it might indeed be a good idea for Bill to adopt them. But the most important point is not what Bill writes but how the reader – in this case Carole – interprets his message. Conflict is initiated less by other people's behaviour than by how we read that behaviour, and how quickly we make negative judgements. In fact, there are many positive aspects to Bill's email. How many of these did you see?

Positive intent

Bill discusses a problem proactively. Perhaps he is motivated by openness and honesty.

Results-orientated

Bill clearly wants to get results both internationally and in his local office.

People-focused

Bill is protecting Jacques. This may be from a sense of organisational responsibility (Jacques has a talent that needs to be nurtured), but it may also be motivated by another positive quality – loyalty.

Closed dialogue

The email stays private. There is no escalation of the issue through the involvement of another party. So discretion seems to be another of Bill's positive qualities.

Diplomacy

Bill's email is quite diplomatic. Nothing in it necessarily communicates any sense of blame or personal attack. He keeps to the facts and invites further dialogue to resolve differences of opinion.

In fact, there is not a single sentence in Bill's email that we cannot interpret as having a positive intention. So, in finding faults with this email and suggesting improvements, we may be guilty of making unfair assumptions about Bill's motives. In other words, we may be the real generators of conflict by email.

This leads us to three tips for reading emails:

1 **Don't react too quickly**
   When you judge something negatively, you are probably imposing your own values on the situation. Remember this when you feel negative emotions appearing. Start the habit of rereading the emails you receive.

2 **Read positive intention**
   Look for any positives, even in emails that seem to attack you (or others). This allows you to respond more positively. There will nearly always be positives if you are open enough to spot them.

3 **Think beyond the person and think about processes**
   Emails that discuss problems may be a sign of organisational difficulties. (Jacques is involved in two projects, which may mean that the company lacks resources.) Look at the possible systemic issues behind a conflict and try not to see everything as a clash of personalities.

Developing your email skills

Take a look at some of the emails that you have written recently and see how effectively you built relationships, influenced people and managed conflict. Then try to integrate some of the ideas from this unit into your future emails. Also, monitor the emails that you receive as a way of assessing the success of your communication. If you continue this process over a period of time, you should find yourself writing more sensitively and effectively – and achieving better business results.

What do you write?

Building relationships

Here are some ideas on how to write emails to affiliation-oriented individuals. The strategies will differ, depending on whether you are initiating an email exchange or replying to an email.

	Sending	Replying to an email
Creating a positive feeling at the start of the email	*I hope you're well.* *Hope you're having a good week.*	*Many thanks for your email.* *Good to hear from you.*
Focusing on news	*I've been travelling a lot.* *Life is pretty busy at the moment.*	*Interesting to hear your news.* *Hope things are not too busy.*
Showing appreciation	*Many thanks in advance for this.* *Your help is much appreciated.*	*Many thanks for your support.* *I really appreciate your help.*
Looking forward positively	*Looking forward to hearing from you.* *Speak to you tomorrow.*	*Hope this helps.* *Get back to me if you need more.*

As a relationship develops, the style of English can become more informal and conversational. It is also important to recognise when others use this style with you, and to be able to adapt your style towards theirs. Here are some examples of a more informal style, but you can also keep a record of useful phrases that you read in other people's emails and integrate them into your own.

Asking for help
- *Is there any chance that you could ...*
- *Could you do me a favour? I need ...*

Offering support
- *Just let me know if you need me to ...*
- *I'm happy to give you some help if you need it.*

Suggesting contact
- *Call me tomorrow sometime.*
- *I'll phone you in the afternoon.*

Asking for contact
- *Could you get in touch after ...?*
- *We need to make contact before ...*

Influencing people: building clear messages through clear structure

Here are three examples of good structures:

1 Introduction, problem, recommendation and reason

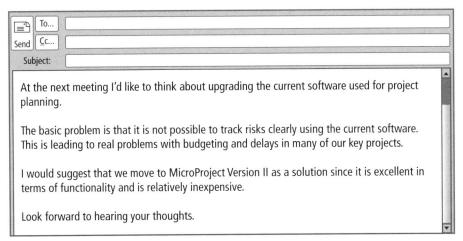

At the next meeting I'd like to think about upgrading the current software used for project planning.

The basic problem is that it is not possible to track risks clearly using the current software. This is leading to real problems with budgeting and delays in many of our key projects.

I would suggest that we move to MicroProject Version II as a solution since it is excellent in terms of functionality and is relatively inexpensive.

Look forward to hearing your thoughts.

2 From experience to proposal

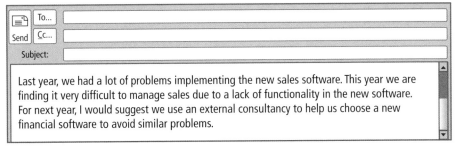

Last year, we had a lot of problems implementing the new sales software. This year we are finding it very difficult to manage sales due to a lack of functionality in the new software. For next year, I would suggest we use an external consultancy to help us choose a new financial software to avoid similar problems.

3 Historical analysis as a basis for decision making

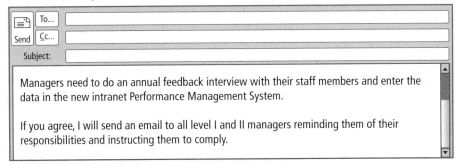

Managers need to do an annual feedback interview with their staff members and enter the data in the new intranet Performance Management System.

If you agree, I will send an email to all level I and II managers reminding them of their responsibilities and instructing them to comply.

Using linking language to structure your message

Linking language helps to build strong and powerful arguments. Here are some examples:

Function	Examples
Sequencing	*firstly, secondly, thirdly, after that, finally*
Adding	*in addition, moreover, furthermore*
Alternatives	*alternatively, instead of*
Consequence	*therefore, consequently*
Comparing	*similarly, in line with*
Contrasting	*however, yet, whereas, although, despite*
Conditions	*if, on condition that, providing, unless*
Reference	*with respect to, regarding, in relation to*
Reasons	*because, since, as, in response to*
Cause verbs	*to lead to, to result in, to bring about, to cause*
Effect verbs	*to result from, to be due to, to be caused by*
Highlighting	*in particular, especially, mainly, chiefly*
Exemplifying	*for example, for instance, such as, as follows*
Generalising	*usually, normally, in general*

Influencing people: Creating an interactive and engaging message

Be open to questions and comment
- *If you have any questions, please contact me.*
- *It would be good to have your feedback on this.*

Use both email and the phone
- *I'll call you tomorrow to discuss this.*
- *I think it would be useful to talk about this by phone.*

Offer a follow-up call
- *If you would like to talk through this, I'll be happy to give you a call.*
- *Please call me if you would like to discuss ...*

Managing conflict

Mix criticism in with praise ('positive framing')
- *You've done a great job with ...*
- *However, one thing I would like to discuss with you is ...*
- *The results last year were good, but what we need to talk about is ...*

Be explicit about what you are *not* saying to reduce the potential for negative interpretation
- *I'm certainly not saying that ... But I would like to ...*
- *Please don't see this as a criticism because ... But I think ...*

Make clear that you are expressing a view, not stating facts
- *I know this may not be your opinion, but from my perspective ...*
- *I think we need to think about how others may see this and so we may need to ...*

13 TELEPHONING

Connecting people

> Advertising slogan of Nokia, Finnish multinational communications corporation

In every modern office you see people sitting at their desks or standing in corridors with their mobile phones. But what are they doing? Quite often they are not talking but rather reading their emails and sending text messages. The telephone is being used more and more now for exchanging text. This is a pity because speaking over the phone to someone has many advantages over written communication.

In this unit we make the case for a more intensive and targeted use of the telephone, with tips on specific language and communication strategies.

Before you read on, think about these questions:

1 Why do people often prefer to send an email rather than phone?
2 What is the best way to start a call?
3 What makes a good voicemail message?
4 What is the right way to deal with customer complaints?

Phone or email?

There are a number of good reasons why people prefer to send an email rather than use the phone:

1 Telephone calls often have to be scheduled, which can be complicated. It can seem simpler to send an email and let people reply in their own time. Indeed, this makes sense when you are just asking for information, as people may need time to find the information you want.

2 Speaking on the phone is much more challenging for many non-native speakers than the relative safety of email. This is particularly true if the person on the other end of the phone has a strong accent or speaks very fast or unclearly (or all three!). Telephoning is also more difficult if the other person has a low level of English.

3 Email allows you to document what you are saying and therefore keep other people informed. This can be very important when there is conflict or disagreement. What was said and promised during a telephone call can be disputed, but the contents of an email are there for anyone to see.

So what are the three big advantages of picking up your phone and calling someone?

1 It's personal

Talking to people on the phone generally offers better opportunities for relationship building than email. You hear their voices and you have at least a chance of reading their feelings. You can spend time listening to their problems. You can convince others that you take an interest in them in a way that is not so easy by email. And because a call is (probably) not being recorded, you can be more open with your own feelings than you might be in an email.

2 It's immediate

Communication should be more efficient on the telephone. We can clarify as we speak. We can put things another way if people do not understand us the first time. We can check whether people understand with quick follow-up questions. In theory, we can do all of this by email, but it sometimes take days to reach an understanding by email while we can reach the same understanding in a telephone call in minutes.

3 It offers added value

Emails tend to be more focused than telephone calls. When we talk on the phone, we can discuss other topics, gossip, and catch up on other subjects that may have an impact on our work.

Think about your main communication channels at work. How much time do you give to each? Should you be allocating your time differently?

Managing the medium

Talking on the phone is very similar to talking face-to-face. But there are some features of the telephone that mean we have to use specific communication and language strategies.

1 Getting connected

The first challenge is the basic one of getting connected to the right person. This may not seem to be an issue in the age of mobile phones. Surely you can simply dial the number and the right person will answer. Unfortunately there are two scenarios that are more challenging:

You have to connect via another person

Imagine that you have to make a call to a new contact, and have to go via a third person – a personal assistant or the company switchboard. If the third person's English skills are not strong, and the pronunciation of your name – or that of the person you wish to speak to – is problematic, getting connected may be challenging. Minimise any difficulties by making sure you:

- can pronounce the name of your contact clearly
- know the title and department of the person; this will help the switchboard understand who you want to talk to
- can say and spell your name slowly and clearly. Be tolerant if the person makes mistakes.

Personal assistants act as gatekeepers for their managers. If you are ringing with a scheduled appointment, you will probably be put through quite quickly. If you are calling without an appointment, you may need to promote yourself more strongly.

You have to leave a message

It is important when leaving a message to be concise (try to keep the message below 30 seconds), to be clear about how urgent the issue is, and to suggest what should happen next (who calls whom, on which number and when). You can find a sample voicemail message in the *What do you say?* section at the end of this unit.

2 Starting up

The style of introduction – whether you are making or answering a call – depends on a number of factors.

Cultural context and individual preferences

Some people use only their family name to identify themselves when they pick up the phone. Others may use a formula designed by their organisation to promote an image of good customer service.

The relationship between the people

Callers introduce themselves to another person in a style that characterises their professional relationship, either formal or less formal. With caller ID display, the person calling may not need – or have the opportunity – to make an introduction. The receiver often knows who is calling and can greet the caller immediately.

Checking if someone is free to talk

With an unscheduled call, and even sometimes with scheduled calls, it is important to check if the person is available to talk.

Rescheduling

Calls frequently have to be rescheduled due to unforeseen events or office pressures. Be prepared for this and do not judge it as a sign of inefficiency in your counterpart.

Small talk or down to business?

We have the same dilemma on the phone as when meeting face-to-face: how much time should we invest in small talk, and when should we get down to business? Choose a style that is appropriate for the person you are talking to and the context. If there is an emergency, you will obviously not spend hours discussing the weather. However, it may be helpful with international contacts to first ask a few polite questions to create a positive atmosphere for the discussion.

Agreeing the purpose of the call

As with face-to-face meetings, it is important to clarify the purpose and process of the phone call. If the call has been scheduled and an agenda set in an email, this can be referred to and agreed in very much the same way as in a meeting.

3 During the call

Telephone communication is more challenging because we do not usually have the visual supports that help us to assess what someone is really saying, how strongly they feel, how far they agree with an idea, etc. This makes it important to activate many of the communication principles outlined in the first two units of this book.

Keep It Short and Simple (KISS)

When speaking on the phone, keep your messages short. Also, make clear the reasons for your message so that people can understand why you are saying what you are saying.

Check

When listening, we need to clarify a lot in order to check our understanding.

Move on

If we rely simply on someone's voice, it can be difficult to hear when it is time to move to the next topic or whether people want to keep talking about the current issue. This needs to be explicitly clarified.

4 Closing the call

As with face-to-face communication, it is important to handle well the transition from discussion to the end of the conversation. For example, you can use a simple phrase like *So, is there anything else?* Also, take the time to summarise the call and to list any actions that have been agreed.

Very often people end calls too quickly because they want to end the stressful experience! But after summarising, use the opportunities that a telephone contact can offer, particularly with colleagues who are overseas:

- Find out about other relevant issues.
- Ask about what is going on in the local organisation.
- Look for opportunities to expand your network.

Technical problems

Various technical problems can arise with telephone communication. It is important to be able to deal with them decisively and clearly, in order to avoid wasting time or creating an unprofessional impression. What would you say in the following situations and what solution would you offer? Compare your answers with the answers in the answer key.

- You cannot hear the other person very well.
- There is an echo: you can hear your own voice speaking as you speak.
- Your phone battery is very low.
- The network signal for your mobile phone is low.
- You call a person back after the phone conversation was cut off.

Complaints and customer service

One of the most challenging telephone situations is dealing with an angry customer who wants to make a complaint. Here are some basic guidelines:

The buck stops here

Accept personal responsibility because, for the customer, you *are* your company or organisation.

Admit the mistake

Do not try to defend yourself or your organisation, even if you think you are right. If the customer feels something has gone wrong, then it has! There are two key rules for dealing with customers. Rule one: the customer is always right. Rule two: if the customer is wrong, see rule one!

Apologise and empathise

Make sure that the customer knows you understand the inconvenience caused, and that you sympathise with him or her. Do not be afraid to apologise. That does not mean that you are admitting to some personal mistake. Practise saying sorry!

Act now

Do what you can immediately to start the process of putting things right. If it is impossible to deal with the problem straightaway, get agreement on a clear time frame.

Offer compensation

Some small compensation is often enough to satisfy a customer. It shows that you value the business they are bringing to you and that you are interested in a long-term relationship.

Thank the customer

Surveys show that for every customer who complains, there are more than twenty 'silent sufferers'. So you should be grateful for the feedback that this one is giving you, even if it is expressed negatively.

Pick up the phone

Modern business culture has become too dependent on email and text as means of communication, despite all their advantages. It is time to pick up the phone and start talking to people again. This needs careful time management. It also means developing more confidence with your English, and thinking carefully about the appropriate communication strategies. But the telephone can offer real benefits in professional communication and, if used properly, can create strong foundations for trust and effective cooperation.

What do you say?

Starting the call

Answering the phone
- *Becker* (surname only: this can seem abrupt to people from cultures where it is usual to give two names)
- *Peter Hartley. How can I help you?*
- *Hello, Idris. How are you?* (when you can see the caller's ID)

Introducing yourself as the caller (different styles)
- *Good morning. This is Jean-Paul calling from the Paris office.*
- *Hey, David. It's Elio. How are things?*

Identifying yourself using a company formula
- *This is Standard Insurance, accident claims department. My name is Stuart Wilson. How can I help you?*

Connecting via a third person
- *Hi, it's Geert Hansen here from the Denmark office. That's spelt H-A-N-S-E-N.*
- *May I speak to Mr Meier, the head of marketing?*
- *We just had some email correspondence and I need to give him some figures urgently.*

Checking if the person is free to talk
- *Do you have a few moments?*
- *Is this a good time to talk?*

Rescheduling
- *Sorry, Sasha, but can I call you back? I have Georg on the other line.*
- *Could we postpone to tomorrow? I'm very busy at the moment.*

Small talk or down to business?
- *Good to hear from you. How are you?*
- *So, how's life in Milan? Are you very busy at the moment?*
- *Nice to talk to you again. How's the weather where you are?*
- *How's the weather in Australia? I saw you had a lot of rain.*

Stating the reason for the call
- *I'm calling / ringing / phoning to …*
- *The reason I called is to …*

Referring to an agenda sent by email
- *Do you have the agenda from my email yesterday in front of you?*
- *So, as I said in the email, I'd like to …*

Defining the process
- *So, as I said in the email, I'd like to review the status of the project with you. And then I have some information about a new software update which you need to know. Is there anything else we need to discuss today?*

During the call

Speaking directly
- *To put it simply, I think we need to …*
- *I'm not saying this to criticise. I want to help you to …*

Clarifying as a listener
- *So, you mean that …*
- *So, just to summarise, we agree to …*

Asking for clarification as to whether to move on
- *Do you want to discuss this more or can we move on to the next topic?*

Managing the agenda
- *Is that everything on …?*
- *Do you want to say more on this or shall we move on to …?*

Keeping the message short
- *So, to put it simply, I think we need to …*

Closing the call

Signalling that the call is finishing
- *So, is there anything else?*
- *Can we summarise now?*

Summarising
- *So, to summarise, the next step is to …*
- *So, we agreed to …*

Asking additional questions
- *While I have you on the line, I have a question about …*
- *Oh, just one thing I wanted to ask you …*

Finding out the latest events in other organisations
- *How's life in Barcelona? Is the change process going well?*
- *Has Jan left the company? I heard that he was thinking of …*

Expanding your network
- *Is there anyone else who I should / could talk to about this*
- *Do you know anyone who might be interested in …?*
- *Do you know …? I'd like to organise a meeting with her about this. Can you help?*

Closing politely
- *Nice talking to you.*
- *Thanks for calling.*

Ending with future reference
- *Speak to you again soon. Goodbye.*
- *See you next week. Bye.*

Complaints and customer service

The buck stops here
- *Let me help you with this.*
- *I'll see to it that this is dealt with immediately.*
- *I can sort this out for you.*

Admit the mistake
- *I see the problem.*
- *I see the difficulty here.*
- *There's clearly been a mistake.*
- *There must have been a misunderstanding here.*

Apologise and empathise
- *I'm very sorry about this. It must have caused you a few problems.*
- *I really do apologise. This must have been very annoying.*
- *I understand that this must have been very upsetting. I'm sorry.*

Act now
- *I'll get on to this right away and I'll get back to you in ten minutes.*
- *Our technician is out at the moment, but I'll get him to call you before twelve. Is that OK?*
- *Mr Ronzoni should be able to help you. Let me put you through to him and I'll explain the urgency of the situation to him.*

Offer compensation
- *I'll send you a voucher for €100.*
- *Naturally, we'll cover the shipping costs.*
- *Please accept this small gift to make up for all the inconvenience.*

Thank the customer
- *Thanks for letting us know about this.*
- *Thank you for bringing this to our attention.*
- *Thank you very much for the information and for your understanding.*

Your voicemail message: sample
- *I am not available at the moment. Please leave your name and number, and a short message, and I will call you back as soon as I can. Thank you.*

Leaving a voicemail: sample
- *Hello Dan, it's Tomoji. I'm calling about your email this morning to confirm that I am available next Tuesday for a conference call as suggested. I do have ideas on the agenda but prefer to discuss by phone. Can you give me a call back sometime this afternoon between 3 and 6 on my mobile? If not, let me have some times by email when I can call you. Thanks. Talk soon.*

14 TAKING PART IN CONFERENCE CALLS

Researchers find that attendees of business video conferences must work harder to interpret information delivered during a conference call than they would if they attended face-to-face meetings.

Wikipedia, web-based, collaborative encyclopedia, launched 2001

Telephone and video conferences are now a key part of international business life, especially for people working in international teams.

In this unit we focus mainly on the challenge of telephone conference calls or virtual meetings, and suggest ways to make them work better. We will also give you tips on how to handle the specific challenges of virtual meetings when using video conferencing technology. Before you read on, think about these questions:

Q
1 What can you do to prepare effectively for conference calls?

2 What's the best way to start a conference call?

3 What techniques can help you lead virtual meetings effectively?

4 What is good etiquette for participants in virtual meetings?

Preparing

To be successful, conference calls need effective planning. The first step is to decide on the right mix of virtual and face-to-face meetings for the people involved. For example, face-to-face meetings every few months may be necessary to maintain trust and to help with effective information exchange.

The second step concerns the purpose of conference calls, deciding what can be achieved in a virtual environment. Difficult decisions or conflicts are probably best dealt with offline, on a one-to-one or one-to-two basis, and then reported back to the larger group. Conference calls involving larger numbers of people are best suited to updating, briefing, and relatively simple decisions about goals and actions.

Getting the logistics right is critical to the success of conference calls:

1 People

It may be helpful to talk to people individually before the call to discuss the objectives and desired outcomes. Of course this is also helpful for face-to-face meetings, but it is even more important for conference calls as there is less opportunity for clarification of viewpoints.

2 Organisation

- When announcing the conference call via email, make sure the timing is clear to everyone, particularly when people are in different time zones.
- If the meeting is longer than 90 minutes, plan breaks to keep people fresh and inform people of these in advance.

3 Technology

- Make sure that you are familiar with the conference call environment and technology.
- Check that all necessary login and passwords have been sent and received.
- Log in to the conference call five or ten minutes before the official start time to check that everything is working.
- Advise people on potential quality problems in advance. Be aware that some telephone conferencing systems lose quality when people dial in using a mobile or cordless phone.
- Have a back-up plan in case of serious technical problems. For example, have alternative dial in / log in numbers in case of connection problems.

4 Information

- Create an agenda that is clear about the outcomes, process, timing and roles.
- Send participants the agenda and supporting documents well in advance and tell them which documents will be used or referred to at which point in the meeting.
- Translate important documents for people whose English may not be good.
- Number all documents so that it is easy to refer to them during the call.

Getting started

The person leading or facilitating the meeting should enter the virtual environment first and to be ready to welcome the others as they arrive. Most telephone conference calls indicate if you are first into the conference. If this is not indicated, you know that other people are already present.

As people log in, the chair can initiate small talk or informal introductions between participants, if numbers allow for this: with a large number of participants it may be difficult. Participants should make sure that their arrival is noted by the chair and then say a few words of introduction. These opening moments can be chaotic, particularly on telephone conference calls, so saying less rather than more can help the chair to keep control.

Tips for successful chairing

- Set the right tone for the meeting with positive comments to participants.
- Introduce early arrivals to later arrivals as a team-building activity.
- Do formal introductions of new members.
- For telephone conference calls, a roll call (checking that people are present person by person) is useful to make clear who is at the meeting
- Check and then deal with technical problems.
- Find out if anyone has to leave early so you know whether the order of the points on the agenda will work or not.
- Ensure that the objectives of the meeting are clear.
- Review and amend the agenda as necessary.
- Clarify any rules at the start to ensure an efficient process (see the box below).
- Start the discussion and then invite people by name to take part. Start with people who are likely to show a positive attitude.

> ### 'Rules' for virtual meeting communication
>
> As with face-to-face meetings, defining rules will help an international group to interact more successfully. Here are some suggestions:
>
> 1 Announce names before giving an opinion – particularly important in telephone conference calls.
> 2 Indicate to whom a question is addressed.
> 3 Give everyone the chance to speak.
> 4 Accept the chairperson's authority to interrupt.
> 5 Ask everyone to speak clearly.

Managing the discussion

The choice of approach for conference calls depends very much on the number of participants and the objectives. Typically, the more participants there are present, and the more it is a briefing event, the more directive the chairing style has to be. In smaller groups, a more facilitating style which encourages interaction, may be appropriate. Of course, both styles may be adopted by the chairperson during the same meeting at different times.

1 The directive style

When chairpersons use a directive style, they tend to:
- narrow the scope of the discussion to save time
- use closed questions to produce short answers (*Does everyone agree?*)
- discourage discussion between participants
- push hard towards decisions by suggesting solutions
- interrupt speakers who talk for a long time.

If you decide to use a more directive style in a virtual meeting, it can be helpful to explain why. Otherwise, some participants may react against what they see as a too authoritarian approach.

2 The empowering style

When chairpersons use an empowering style, they tend to:
- encourage discussion and avoid pushing their own agenda
- encourage creative thinking by asking lots of open questions (*What does everyone think about this?*)
- encourage participants to comment on each others' ideas to reach a group solution
- allow time for people to speak, but interrupt those who speak too much.

3 The value of summarising

Whichever style you adopt, remember that conference calls, particularly telephone-only conferences, place far heavier demands on non-native speakers than face-to-face communication does. So the chairperson must clarify and summarise frequently to make sure that everyone understands what has been said. When running a web-based conference with the option to share documents and applications, it can also be a good idea to write the minutes during the meeting. This makes the results of the discussion transparent to all as the meeting progresses and helps people to clarify or disagree with points more easily.

4 Encouraging participation

Chairpersons in conference calls often have to work extra hard to get everyone to say anything. Here are a number of techniques that can help:
- Use people's names frequently to keep their attention, particularly important during telephone conferences.
- Go round the group occasionally to check the opinions of all participants, or use on-screen polling features in web-based applications;
- Offer breaks so that people can stretch their legs and think about what they want to say.
- Encourage people to use an interactive whiteboard or text box in web conferencing software to post comments for discussion.

The role of the participant: Listening

Listening as a participant during conference calls can be more challenging than in face-to-face meetings. Sound quality can be poor, and visual information is absent in telephone conference calls and reduced in video-based ones. Participants should decide whether to adopt a more proactive or a more reactive listening style, depending on the context of each call.

1 Proactive listening

Proactive listeners use a number of techniques to support communication in virtual meetings. They tend to:
- make acknowledging noises (such as *uh-huh, OK, yes, …*) to indicate understanding and / or agreement
- re-formulate the comments of other people to check understanding
- ask follow-up questions to get more information
- send positive signals to people, even when disagreeing with what they are saying
- suggest ways of discussing the issue more efficiently.

2 Reactive listening

Reactive listeners are more passive. They generally:
- remain silent (thinking: *I don't want to disturb the speaker.*)
- do not spend time summarising other people's ideas (thinking: *If it's understood, why waste time?*)
- do not intervene when the meeting goes off track (thinking: *This is the chair's responsibility.*)
- do not give much positive feedback during the meeting (thinking: *I can give the feedback in a personal call or email later.*)
- do not interrupt (thinking: *I don't want to be impolite.*).

The listening style or combination of styles which you choose will depend a lot on the number of participants and the hierarchical relationships between them. Large numbers and strong hierarchies can make it difficult to use proactive listening strategies, as this may be seen as time-wasting, disruptive and even disrespectful. On the other hand, overusing the reactive style is dangerous because it places all the responsibility for directing and clarifying in the hands of the chair, who may struggle as a non-native speaker of English.

Participant etiquette

- Be punctual. Whatever you normally do, try not to arrive late for a conference call.
- Connect from a quiet location and use the mute button when not speaking to avoid background noise.
- If possible, avoid mobile and cordless phones as they can reduce the quality of the connection.
- Don't multitask if your participation is important: remove other papers from your desk and give the meeting your full attention.

The role of the participant: Speaking

Many of the principles of speaking presented in Unit 1 apply to conference calls. Here are some specific tips to support speaking in virtual meetings:

- Make your voice interesting to listen to, by using a positive tone, varied intonation, the right volume and moderate tempo.
- Remember that it is more difficult to understand complex input in a virtual environment, particularly in telephone conference calls. Make your input more understandable by simplifying wherever possible, structuring the message clearly, and making use of supporting documents with clear references to page numbers.
- Avoid the 'one-way effect' where people listen in silence for long periods. Show your understanding of the views of others and express openness to interruptions so that you create a sense of dialogue.
- Use a clear handover to signal to others that you have stopped speaking and that others may now comment or add opinions.

Sorry to interrupt but ...

Getting the opportunity to speak can be difficult in conference calls, especially with large numbers of participants. Many non-native speakers lack the confidence and sense of timing to interrupt politely. Some see interruption as impolite in principle and remain silent as a sign of respect. Others find it difficult to know when someone is going to stop speaking and whether others also want to interrupt. The result can be domination by the more assertive communicators, often the native speakers.

It is important, therefore, to practise some simple phrases to interrupt, such as *Sorry to interrupt but …* or *I agree with that, and I'd like to add that ….* It is probably best to avoid using the expression *Yes, but …,* as this may sound negative.

Closing

Allow more time than in face-to-face meetings for explicit summarising and checking. Participants with lower levels of English competence in particular will welcome the opportunity to go over decisions again.

If you are leading a virtual meeting, you should follow up with a personal telephone call to anyone who you think may not have understood the decisions or who is not fully committed to them. This form of post-meeting management is essential for virtual meetings because it is easier for participants to hide their disagreement and lack of commitment by simply saying nothing.

Improve your conference calls

Take a few minutes at the end to do after-call feedback. The chair can either request feedback directly or can send an email request after the meeting. This creates opportunities to clarify issues and also produces a more open conference-call culture. Alternatively, you could use a more formal feedback sheet similar to this feedback sheet.

Conference call feedback sheet

Score your answer to each question on a scale of 1–5 (1 completely unacceptable, 2 unsatisfactory, 3 satisfactory, 4 good, 5 excellent)

1 How well was the conference call facilitated?

   How could facilitation be improved?

   ◯

2 How good was the technology?

   How could we improve how we use it?

   ◯

3 How effective was the interaction between participants?

   How could we improve it?

   ◯

4 How well did you understand the discussion?

   How could we improve understanding?

   ◯

5 What other ideas do you have to improve our conference calls?

Prepare for the future

Virtual working is increasing and will probably be the commonest form of interaction between professionals working in global teams for large international organisations in the future. The skills you need to lead and interact in virtual meeting environments – both audio and video – are evolving all the time. It is therefore important that you have a plan to improve your virtual communication skills to meet this new challenge.

What do you say?

Getting started

Arriving at the conference call
- *Hello, John from London here.*

Welcome
- *Welcome to the meeting.*

Introducing early arrivals to each other
- *Carlos, can I introduce you to Rob? He's from the Sydney office.*

Roll call
- *Before we start, I'd like to check that everyone is here and that the technology is working.*

Asking for introductions
- *Would you like to introduce yourself to the others?*

Introducing others
- *Let me say a few words about Hans-Peter.*

Making formal introductions of new members
- *I'd like to start by welcoming Andres from Barcelona to the meeting today. He's here as a finance expert and will be talking us through the business case in more detail later. Andres, would you like to say anything?*

Review protocol
- *I propose that people introduce themselves before they speak. Please keep comments short and focused, and ask questions directly to named individuals.*

State dos
- *Please feel free to speak when you want to say something.*
- *Tell me if you are having problems saying what you want to say.*
- *Ask for clarification if there are any parts of the discussion you don't understand.*

State don'ts
- *Please don't interrupt others if you can avoid it.*

Clarify minutes
- *Anna will be typing the minutes on screen as we go.*

Check personal schedules
- *Does anyone have to leave the meeting early? If so, when?*

Technical issues
- *Can you all hear me OK?*
- *Can you all see the slide on the screen?*
- *Are there any technical problems?*
- *I think there's a technical problem. The slide isn't displaying.*
- *Can you log out and in again and see if that helps?*
- *Can you move a little closer to the microphone?*
- *Can you move the camera a little? It's pointing at …*

- *The connection is bad. Could you dial in again?*
- *The dial-in number / password isn't working.*
- *Could you try … instead and see if that works?*

Participating

Announce your name before you speak
- *Jon, from Maryville, USA. I'd like to say that …*

Use other people's names
- *As John said earlier, …*

Indicate to whom a question is addressed
- *This is Yasmin Dalindyebo, and this question is for Michaela Seale.*

Signal when you want to hand over
- *So that's all I wanted to say on that. Back to you, Misha.*

Comment
- *John, Hans-Peter here. That's a good point.*

Ask for clarification
- *John, it's Hans-Peter. What do mean by …?*

Ask for repetition
- *I'm sorry, could you repeat that, Jan?*

Reformulate
- *If I understand you correctly, you want to …*

Show agreement
- *Mario, it's Misha. Can I just say how much I agree because …*

Request more
- *Klaus, could you say a little more about that?*

Interrupt
- *It's Gudrun. Sorry for interrupting but can I come in here?*

Add
- *Sorry, John. Can I add something?*

Stop an interruption
- *Pia, could I just finish and then I'll hand over?*

Support protocol
- *Could everyone say their name before speaking? It's a little confusing at the moment.*
- *I think it would be better if people made their inputs shorter.*
- *Elio, could we take a short time out as I need to deal with something here in the office?*

Make the communication clear by introducing comments with the name of the person speaking and the name of the person who spoke just before.

Managing the discussion

Show your understanding of the views of others
• *Just to build on what some of you were saying, …*

Give everyone a chance to speak
• *Please can we hear from someone in southern Europe. Elio?*

Accept the chairperson's authority to interrupt
• *Xavier, sorry to interrupt. Can I remind you of the agreed rules? Please ask a question to a named person and not just openly to the group.*

The directive style

Say what style you plan to adopt at the beginning, especially if there is a large number of participants:

I plan to be quite strict and focused for today's call because this virtual format is not best for long discussions, and we only have 45 minutes. I propose to note any major open questions and deal with them at the next meeting.

Get opinion	*Hans-Peter, what do you think about this?*
Focus the discussion	*Thanks for that, John. I think we need to decide …*
Check agreement	*Jens, do you agree with this?*
Involve others	*I'd like to hear John's views now. John?*
Postpone	*I think we should deal with this next time. OK, Peter?*
Stop digression	*Can we come back to the agenda? Peter, …*
Hurry people up	*Can we speed this up a little? We're very short of time.*
Stress simplicity	*Everyone, please keep inputs as simple as possible.*
Slow people down	*Adriana, could you slow down a little? I think some people are having problems following you.*
Ask for more volume	*Please speak up a little, John.*
Clarify long inputs	*John, can I interrupt you a moment to clarify … OK, is that clear to everyone, starting with Anna. Was that clear, Anna? … (pause) … Hans-Peter? … (pause)*
Stop an interruption	*Sorry, John. Can you let Anna finish?*
Move on	*OK. The next point is …*
Make a decision	*Let's take a decision on this. I propose that we …*
Agree decision	*OK. Can we go quickly round the group? Please say 'yes' if you agree. Peter? … (pause) … Misha? … (pause)*
Summarise decision	*Then we agree to …*

Notice how names are used to signal who is being spoken to and who should speak next.

The empowering style

Ask for opinions	*What do people think about this? Any comments?*
Ask for comment	*Does anyone want to comment on Hans-Peter's position?*
Ask for proposals	*Are there any suggestions as to how to deal with this problem?*
Asks open questions	*How far do people think that we can …*
Asks for decision	*Would anyone like to comment further?*

Closing

Minuting in real time	*Can everyone see the minutes on screen? Are there any comments or changes, or can we accept these and close?*
Feedback (directive)	*Before we close, I'd like to make a few comments about the efficiency of the meeting.*
Feedback (facilitating)	*Would anyone like to say anything about the efficiency of the meeting?* *Can we do anything better for the next conference call?*
Feedback after the meeting (by email)	*How did we do?* *What worked well and what didn't work so well?*

15 WORKING IN VIRTUAL TEAMS

> **Out of sight, out of mind.**
>
> Thomas à Kempis, German Catholic monk and writer (1380–1471)

As discussed in earlier units, professional people are finding themselves working more and more in virtual teams. Team members in different locations rely more and more on electronic channels of communication such as video and audio conferencing (see Unit 14). Virtual teams may also use professional and social networking technologies such as Wikis or team Facebook sites to distribute and share information.

Virtual team workers do not have the regular opportunities for chats by the coffee machine and unplanned meetings in the corridor which members of face-to-face teams have. They often face the additional challenges associated with working in multinational organisations. These include greater cultural diversity and problems communicating across time zones.

In this final unit we summarise the major challenges of working in a virtual team and give you the opportunity to rate your skills. Before you read on, think about these three questions:

1 How can you build trust in a virtual team?

2 When should virtual team members communicate electronically, and when is it necessary to communicate face-to-face?

3 Which communication skills are particularly important for members of virtual teams?

4 What can members of virtual teams do to manage their time effectively when working under a lot of pressure?

What people say about virtual teams

Despite the everyday challenges of working in a teams whose members are all at the same location, it seems that people generally prefer face-to-face teams to virtual ones. Look at these typical comments made by professionals about their experience of working virtually. Which statements do you agree with most and are closest to your views? Why?

About relationships

> I have to work with this guy and I know nothing about him. I don't even know if he's competent.

> It's difficult to build trust with someone you only meet twice a year.

About communication

> He never replies to my emails.

> You can't have a useful discussion during a telephone conference with more than ten people.

About leadership

> I find it difficult to get people to deliver on time.

> I have the problem of managing local managers who put team members under pressure to put local priorities before my team's goals.

The good virtual worker

What characteristics do you need to be an effective virtual worker? In this section, we provide some suggestions and give you the opportunity to rate your skills.

1 Good technical skills

It is important for virtual team members to be familiar with all types of technology, including video and audio conferencing platforms, group database systems, and new software and networking technologies that can be used to plan and record team work. Particularly useful is the ability to troubleshoot and solve the irritating glitches that can arise during conference calls.

But virtual team workers should not be over-technical. It is also important to know when to use which technology, and when not to use technology at all and instead set up a face-to-face meeting. This can be particularly important for discussions of sensitive or complex issues.

2 The ability to work independently

Being a member of a virtual team means working without regular supervision. A higher level manager is no longer walking past your desk every day to check on what you are doing. So effective virtual workers need to be independent, motivated self-starters who can work hard and deliver high quality without being given lots of instructions. They need the tolerance to accept that changing project targets may mean that they have to throw away what they have done and start again. They also need to be able to take leadership responsibilities and to be proactive in foreseeing and solving problems.

3 Good time management skills

Virtual workers need to be excellent time managers who can prioritise local and virtual team tasks effectively and meet their deadlines. They should communicate their work status regularly to relevant managers, and reply promptly to emails to avoid senders wondering when their urgent email is going to be answered. Time management also means setting time aside for other things in life: to take training courses to bring relevant new skills into the team, to have a life outside work, to reflect and to relax.

Rate your time management competence

1 (low) 2 3 4 5 (high)

I prioritise local and virtual team tasks effectively. ○

I communicate work status regularly. ○

I respond promptly to emails. ○

I make time to relax and for life outside work. ○

4 Good team skills

Although virtual team members need to be strongly independent, they must also know when to support and cooperate with others in the team in order to reach common goals. They should show explicitly that they are ready to help others and to share information. This helps to create a supportive environment and encourages the development of trust.

Good virtual team workers also make efforts to learn about the other members of their team, to appreciate the challenges of their working environments, and to get to know their areas of competence and possible weaknesses. This requires a lot of communication (for example, via email and telephone calls), taking the time to ask questions and listen to others. The time that is invested in this relationship building may seem to offer little value in the short term, but it will enable the team to perform more effectively in the longer term.

Finally, as team players, effective virtual workers try to make life easier for others. They avoid causing extra work, and volunteer to take on additional tasks themselves. Above all, they do not blame or criticise other team members when things go wrong. They appreciate that different working styles are good for teamwork, and seek to exploit the advantages of diversity as much as possible.

Rate your team player skills

1 (low) 2 3 4 5 (high)

I like to help others and share information. ○

I try to learn about others and their contexts. ○

I make time for relationship building. ○

I have a positive attitude to diversity in the team. ○

5 Good communication skills

Above all, effective virtual workers are good communicators. They give the right information at the right level of detail at the right time. Too much or too little information can create stress and confusion. This does not mean that 'Keeping It Short and Simple' (KISS) is always the right approach. Sometimes it can be important to say more than usual, to make explicit your assumptions and intentions. This enables others to understand you better and respond appropriately.

Those leading virtual meetings need to communicate extensively both before the meeting (to assess attitudes and levels of engagement) as well as after the meeting (to assess levels of understanding and commitment to the decisions taken, and to get feedback). Not doing this with key participants poses a real risk to the effectiveness of team decision-making.

Finally, remember that distance reduces the opportunities for informal communication, and for saying what is going well in the team and what needs to be improved. When leading a virtual team, it is important to create a range of opportunities for people to give and get feedback on the team's performance, from one-to-one calls, to brainstorming team improvements together.

Rate your communication skills

1 (low) 2 3 4 5 (high)

I give information at the right level at the right time. ◯

I state explicitly my assumptions and intentions. ◯

I discuss agendas before, and decisions after meetings. ◯

I create a range of opportunities to give and get feedback. ◯

And finally ...

Working effectively in a virtual team, and helping the team to work as a team, needs commitment from everyone involved. All too often, people do not show that commitment because of work pressure or lack of direct supervision. As a result, their virtual teams become less efficient.

We believe that following the ideas in this final unit, and discussing these ideas within your teams offers you a greater chance of success when communicating internationally in English.

CONCLUSION

" **The important thing is to not stop questioning.**

Albert Einstein, theoretical physicist (1879–1955)

"

It is difficult to draw simple conclusions from what is very complex subject. However, one message which comes from experienced international communicators is surprisingly simple: Just ask more questions.

And there is a clear reason for this simple advice. If we have the courage to ask more questions, we get two very important benefits:

1 We are seen as more open by our international partners, which helps us build better relationships.
2 We learn things that we did not expect to learn. We get better quality information. This better information helps us to achieve better results.

Effective communicators are often very curious. They like to ask lots of questions to understand others and the situation. This helps them to take decisions. But knowledge is never absolute. What we know and find out should only ever be a stepping stone to the next question.

We hope *Effective International Business Communication* will support you on your journey to becoming a more effective international communicator. We hope that it will encourage you to speak and to listen to others more thoughtfully, and that it will help you to understand and be understood better as you work internationally.

ANSWER KEY

Unit 2

What stops us from listening effectively: Analysis

Our ability to listen is affected by three main factors, which are illustrated by what is going wrong in the three dialogues.

1 The message. In the first dialogue, the listener feels that this is not a relevant message. In the second dialogue, the listener is confused by the complexity of the explanation.

2 The speaker. Speakers whose tempo, volume or level of emotion is disturbing for the listener will find it more difficult to get their message across. Some listeners may also pay less attention if the speaker lacks status. This is a factor in the third dialogue, in which the listener wants to involve the team leader rather than waste time discussing a subject with a speaker who is not seen as having responsibility for the issue.

3 The listener. The greatest threat to effective listening is actually the listener. Listeners distort and reject messages in ways that they may not be conscious of. This happens particularly when the speaker's message is seen as a form of criticism or threat, or when the listener is under time pressure (as in the first dialogue). Listeners often undervalue the importance of what is said. As a result, listeners may lose the respect of the speaker: *Hey, he's not listening to me. Who does he think he is?* Also, the listener's ability to see things in new ways and to learn will be reduced.

Unit 3

Lunch for two: Small talk strategies to get the conversation going – feedback

Jean takes the initiative (an important strategy) and asks an opening question (work is a safe topic). She is then quick to follow up with another question that shows some knowledge of the other person's working life. Sam recognises that the questions are not really information-oriented and so keeps his answers short before respectfully handing the conversation back to Jean by returning the question (*How about your work?*). Sam listens actively and positively; he repeats words Jean uses (*Finished?*) and shows empathy (*I can imagine.*) He also introduces a little humour to spice up the conversation (*…we'll have to find you something else to keep you busy*), to keep things light and friendly, and to indicate that the conversation topic is over and it is time to order. Jean responds positively to the humour with an ironic comment (… *thanks very much for that thought*) and is sensitive to the fact that it is time to order.

Summary of strategies for building relationships at first meetings
- Taking the initiative
- Asking a question
- Asking a follow-up question
- Showing knowledge of the other person's working life
- Keeping answers short
- Handing the conversation back by returning a question
- Active and positive listening
- Repeating words which others use
- Showing empathy
- Introducing humour
- Responding to the humour of others positively
- Being sensitive to the need to order (specific to being in a restaurant)

Unit 4

Conversation and group dynamics: An answer

B is the most obvious cluster to approach as the body language from both individuals looks open to a person joining. Cluster A seems locked in a strong conversation. In cluster C, the person on the bottom left of the three may be open to an approach as the body language indicates some awareness of a person entering from the doorway. Person E looks to be walking towards person D but it is not clear if these two people are open to a third person joining as they may know each other and are about to start a private conversation.

Unit 6

Stages in an introduction to a meeting: Answer

Initiate: *OK, shall we get started?*

Welcome: *Firstly, a quick welcome to Jan, who has joined us from the Belgian office. Nice to have you here.*

Role: *Jan will be presenting some figures later when we talk about the new cross-border initiative.*

Agenda: *OK, in terms of agenda, if you all have it in front of you, as you can see, the main objective today is to take a decision on the next phase of the project. Do we feel ready to start, and, if so, when? We'll do an update of progress so far, that's from me. Then I just want to give you some information from the recent leadership meeting in Milan. And then we can talk about the decision and the pros and cons of moving on with things now or waiting.*

Rules: *Just to remind you of a few rules, as always: mobile phones off, and the native English speakers should try to try to speak clearly so that our colleagues from around the world can understand.*

Confirm: *OK?*

Begin: *Good, then let's get started with …*

Unit 8

Test: how impatient are you? Comments

38–50: Your impatience is likely to be causing you and others problems. Try getting feedback from your boss and colleagues about this so that you realise the consequences of your behaviour. Then think seriously about implementing techniques for stronger emotional control.

25–37: You may be in control most of the time, but occasionally you are not operating effectively because your emotions are out of control. Try implementing the ideas in this unit for those situations in which you feel impatience may be a problem.

12–24: You are generally calm and collected. Think about how you can spread your calm to other team members to create a more productive atmosphere.

0–11: You are exceptional! If you know how you do this, then tell your colleagues. They will benefit.

Unit 12

A task-oriented email: Model answer

There is no single correct answer to this question. In the model below, Jackie focuses purely on asking the main question and giving clear (solution-oriented) advice.

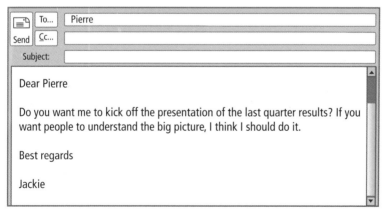

To...	Pierre
Send Cc...	
Subject:	

Dear Pierre

Do you want me to kick off the presentation of the last quarter results? If you want people to understand the big picture, I think I should do it.

Best regards

Jackie

Unit 13

Technical problems: Model answers

You can't hear the other person very well
- *Veronica, I can't hear you very well. Could you speak up a little?*
- *Peter, the line is very bad. I can't hear you. Can you call me back?*

You can hear your own voice speaking as you speak
- *Stefan, there's an echo on the line. I'll call you back.*
- *Sorry, but I can hear myself. Can you call me back and see if we get a better connection?*

Your phone battery is very low
- *Juan, my battery is low so I may cut out. If so, I'll call you back on my landline.*
- *Ahmed, I have almost no battery left. Let me plug in the charger.*

The network signal for your mobile phone is low
- *I have almost no signal. Let's try but it may cut out. If so, I'll call you back.*
- *The network is terrible here. Can I call you later?*

You call back and check if quality has improved

• *Is that better?* • *Can you hear me now?* • *How's that?*	*Yes, much better.* *Yes, perfect.* *It's the same. Can you try to call again?*

REFERENCES

1 Speaking
Turn taking: see Richard Lewis, *When Cultures Collide: Managing Successfully Across Cultures,* (London: Nicholas Brealey Publishing, 1996). See also Trompenaars, Alfons, Hampden-Turner, Charles and Trompenaars, Fons *Riding the Waves of Culture: Understanding Diversity in Global Business*, (New York: McGraw-Hill Intercultural Assessment project (INCA), 1997). – www.incaproject.org/framework.htm

3 Building relationships
Relationship Awareness Theory: developed by Elias Porter, psychologist (1914–87). See for example: E.H. Porter, *Relationship Awareness Theory, Manual of Administration and Interpretation*, ninth edition. (Carlsbad, CA: Personal Strengths Publishing, Inc. 1973, 1996).

Communication and gender: Deborah Tannen, Professor of Linguistics at Georgetown University, USA. See for example: D. Tannen, *Gender and Discourse* (Oxford: Oxford University Press, 1966).

Relationship-building skills: Centre for Intercultural Learning at the Canadian Foreign Service Institute – www.intercultures.ca/cil-cai/overview-apercu-eng.asp?iso=ca

4 Networking
Conversation and group dynamics: see Ivan Misner, David Alexander, Brian Hilliard, *Networking Like a Pro: Turning Connections Into Contacts*, (California: Entrepreneur Media, 2009).

5 Building trust
Trust: Worldwork is a London-based agency responsible for developing The International Profiler (TIP), a questionnaire and feedback tool that has been developed to help managers and professionals understand where they put the behavioural emphasis when working internationally – www.worldwork.biz

6 Making decisions
Decision-making styles: A. Rowe and J. Boulgarides, *Managerial Decision Making: A Guide to Successful Business Decisions*, (New York: MacMillan, 1992).

9 Managing conflict
Stages of team development: Bruce W. Tuckman and Mary Ann C. Jensen, 'Stages of small group development revisited', *Group and Organizational Studies,* 2, (1977) 419–427.

Profiling team members: Myers-Briggs Type Indicator® (MBTI) – www.cpp.com/products/mbti/index.aspx

Profiling team members: Team Management Systems and the Team Management Wheel® of TMS Development International Ltd (TMSDI®) – www.tmsdi.com

READING LIST

This list contains one or two follow-up titles for further reading for each chapter of this book. If you are interested in learning more about the competences you need for working effectively across cultures, then you should read:

Jeremy Comfort and Peter Franklin, *The Mindful International Manager* (Kogan Page, 978-0-749461-97-3).

1 Speaking
Ron Scollon and Suzanne Wong Scollon, *Intercultural Communication: A Discourse Approach* (Blackwell, 978-0-631-22418-1).

Owen Hargie, *Skilled Interpersonal Communication: Research, Theory and Practice* (Routledge, 978-0-415-43204-7).

2 Listening
Nancy Kline, *Time to Think* (Cassell Illustrated, 978-0-706377-45-3).

Mark Brady, *The Wisdom of Listening* (Wisdom Publications, 978-0-861713-55-4).

3 Building relationships
Jerry Richardson, *The Magic of Rapport* (Meta Publications, 978-0-916990-44-2).

Deborah Tannen, *You Just Don't Understand: Women and Men in Conversation* (HarperCollins, 978-0-060959-62-3).

4 Networking
Ivan Misner, David Alexander and Brian Hilliard, *Networking Like a Pro: Turning Connections Into Contacts* (Entrepreneur Press, 978-1-59918-356-5).

Rob Yeung, *Networking: The New Rules* (Marshall Cavendish, 978-1-905736-30-0).

5 Building trust
C. Burke et al., *Trust in Leadership: A Multi-level Review and Integration* (The Leadership Quarterly, 2007) 606–632.

Ivana Marková and Alex Gillespie (eds), *Trust and Distrust: Sociocultural Perspectives* (Information Age Publishing, 978-1-59311-841-9).

6 Making decisions
Scott Plous, *The Psychology of Judgement and Decision-Making* (McGraw-Hill, 978-0-070504-77-6).

7 Influencing
Robert B. Cialdini, *Influence: The Psychology of Persuasion* (Collins, 978-0-061241-89-5).

Joseph O'Connor, *Leading With NLP: Essential Leadership Skills for Influencing and Managing People* (Thorsons, 978-0-722537-67-1).

8 Dealing with 'difficult people'
Robert M. Bramson, *Coping with Difficult People* (Dell, 978-0-440-20201-1).

9 Managing conflict
Roy J. Lewicki, Bruce Barry and David Saunders, *Negotiation: Readings, Exercises and Cases* (Irwin Professional, 978-0-07353-0314).

Max A. Eggert and Wendy Falzon, *The Resolving Conflict Pocketbook* (Management Pocketbooks, 978-1-903776-06-3).

10 Giving and getting feedback
Clive Fletcher, *Appraisal, Feedback and Development: Making Performance Review Work* (Routledge, 978-0-415-44691-4).

Joseph R. Folkman, *The Power of Feedback: 35 Principles for Turning Feedback from Others into Personal and Professional Change* (John Wiley, 978-0-471-99820-4).

11 Writing email: The basics
Paul Emmerson, *Email English* (Macmillan Education, 978-1-405-01294-2).

Nancy Flynn and Tom Flynn, *Writing Effective E-mail* (Kogan Page, 978-0-74943-326-0).

12 Writing email: Advanced
R. L. Trask, *How to Write Effective Emails* (Penguin, 978-0-14101-719-8).

Monica Seeley, *Brilliant Email: How to Win Back Time and Increase Your Productivity* (Pearson, 978-0-27374-255-5).

13 Telephoning
Susan Lowe, *Telephoning* (Delta Publishing, 978-1-900783-79-8).

Bob Dignen and Jon Dyson, *English for Telephoning (Business Minimax)* (York Associates, 978-1-900991-25-4).

14 Taking part in conference calls
Ida Shessel, *74 Tips for Absolutely Great Teleconference Meetings* (Multi-Media Publications, 978-1-895186-86-4).

Ken Taylor, *Fifty Ways to Improve your Telephoning and Teleconferencing Skills* (Summertown Publishing, 978-1-905992-06-5).

15 Working in virtual teams
Richard Lepsinger and Darleen DeRosa, *Virtual Team Success: A Practical Guide for Working and Leading from a Distance* (Pfeiffer, 978-0-470532-96-6).

Ian Fleming, *Virtual Teams Pocketbook* (Management Pocketbooks, 978-1-903776-41-4).

GLOSSARY

Here are definitions for the more difficult words in this book. This Glossary provides definitions for the words as they are used in this book and it does not give all their possible meanings. Learning how to use them will help you to be able to read about and to speak more effectively about the communication issues discussed in the book, and about business communication in general.

a

adjust	adapt, change in order to fit a different situation
adversarial	involving conflict or opposition
advocate	support or speak in favour of an opinion, policy or cause
aggressive	attacking, unpleasantly forceful, using forceful words and actions
acknowledge	show you have noticed or received something
allocate	distribute something, for example work tasks, to one person or a group of people
ambiguous	something that can be explained or interpreted in more than one way; unclear, not precise
anecdote	a short story, especially about something someone has done
anticipate	see what is going to happen; take action to prepare for something
appraise	measure someone's performance at work
appropriate	the correct or acceptable thing to do in a particular situation
arbitration	the process of solving a disagreement or conflict between two or more people or groups of people by helping them to agree to an acceptable solution
arrogant	behaving in a proud or superior manner; showing too much pride in oneself and too little consideration for others
assertive	behaving confidently; not frightened to say what you want or believe
assess	measure the value, quality or importance of something, for example someone's performance at work

assumption	something that you accept as true without question or proof
authoritarian	a form of organisation in which orders come from above and individuals have little independence
aware	a state of knowing or realising something

b

beneficial	helpful, useful, positive
binding	something, for example an agreement, that you have to accept
boost	improve or increase something
breakout	a rest period during a face-to-face meeting or conference call
briefing	instructions or information given to people

c

capacity	the ability to learn something or develop in some way
claim	a statement by someone that something is true but which is not proved
clarify	make clear; make easier to understand
clash	a serious difference of opinion, a conflict
collaboration	when two or more people work together to achieve the same objective
collectivist culture	one in which members see an important part of their identities coming from the group they belong to
combative	keen or ready to fight or argue
commit	promise to do something
competence	the ability to do something well; the mix of attitudes, skills and knowledge you need to do something well
comply	act in line with the rules
concentrate	mentally focus on one important subject and not think about other less important things
conclusion	the belief or opinion you form after thinking about something; the end of something
conference call	(also referred to as an audio conference or informally as a conf call or telco) a telephone call or meeting with more than two people
counter-argument	a view that you put forward to oppose someone else's view
counter-claim	a claim made against another claim

counterpart	someone doing the same job as you or a similar job to you in another organisation or in another part of your organisation; someone who you are communicating with in another office, organisation or country
critical	extremely important

d

damage	harm or spoil something
deference	the quality of having and showing great respect for someone with higher status connected with age, authority, position in an organisation
delegate	give a task to someone below you in the organisation to carry out while keeping responsibility for the task
demotivate	make someone feel like working less hard
direct report	someone who is one level below you in the organisation
directive	giving orders to people without allowing them much freedom of choice
disrespectful	not showing respect
discretion	behaving without causing embarrassment or attracting too much attention
disruptive	causing problems so that it is more difficult for others to get things done
distort	describe a situation or something that has happened in an untrue or misleading way
dominate	exercise control or power or a very strong influence over someone or something

e

egalitarian	treating everyone in the same way; believing that all people are equally important
empathy	the ability to understand someone else's feelings or experiences, and being able to imagine what is like to be in their situation
escalate	involve a more senior manager in a problem or conflict
evasive	answering questions in a way that is not direct or clear, especially because you do not want to give an honest answer
explicit	clear and exact

f

facilitate	to make an action, event or process (like a meeting) easy or easier

findings	something that is discovered or learnt as a result of an inquiry or survey
formulaic	consisting of fixed and repeated groups of words or ideas
formulate	to create or prepare something carefully
foundation	a basis, an idea or set of ideas on which something is based
frustration	a feeling of annoyance or lack of confidence because you cannot achieve what you want

g

gesture	a movement of a part of the body, especially of the hand or head, intended to signal a certain meaning
glitch	a technical problem

h

harmony	an environment in which people work together happily and without conflict
hierarchy	an organisation with levels in which people higher up give orders to people lower down
hostility	aggressive and negative feelings or behaviour directed by one person or group against another

i

impose	force something on someone
individualist culture	one in which members see an important part of their identities coming from themselves rather than from a group
insight	a deeper understanding of something
instinctive	without thinking or reasoning, reacting automatically
integrity	the quality of being honest and having strong moral principles that you follow in what you do
intention	what you propose or plan to do
interface	the place where two or more people, groups, organisations, systems, etc. meet each other
interdependence	when two or more things or people depend on each other
intermediary	someone who acts as a link between two or more other people, teams, organisations, etc.
interpretation	your view or explanation of something
inspirational	something or someone which motivates you to do better

l
lexicographer   a dictionary writer

m
mandatory   compulsory, obligatory, something you have to do

manipulative   controlling or influencing someone or something in an unfair way

mediation   the process of talking to two separate people or groups involved in a disagreement to try to help them to agree or find a solution to their problems

milestone   an important stage or target during the life of a project

misguided   mistaken or wrong because badly judged or based on wrong information

misinterpret   to understand something or someone wrongly

mood   the state of your feelings or mind at a particular time

motivate   make someone want to do something well

mutual   something shared by two or more people

n
norm   a standard of behaviour for a group

o
outlook   the likely future situation

p
pace   speed

participant   a person who takes part in something

patience   the ability to accept delay, annoyance or difficulty without complaining

peer   a person who is at the same level in the organisation as you

perseverance   the process of making continuing efforts to achieve your goal, not giving up

persistence   the process of continuing to do something in spite of difficulties

perspective   a point of view, an attitude

postpone   delay an event and plan or decide that it should happen at a later date or time

pragmatic   solving problems in a way which suits the present conditions, rather than following fixed theories, ideas or rules

preference	a greater interest in one action or person rather than another
prejudice	a dislike or distrust of a person, group, custom, etc., that is based on fear or false information rather than on reason or experience, and that influences one's attitude and behaviour towards them
proficient	very good at doing something
protocol	a set of rules used in a particular business context like a meeting or a conference call; the fixed language expressions that people use in these contexts
provocative	a form of behaviour that is intended to make people become angry, shocked, surprised, annoyed, etc.
purchaser	someone who buys something
purpose	an intention, an aim or a function of something; a reason for doing something
pushy	(informal and negative) trying to draw attention to yourself; being openly ambitious; dominating

r

receptive	willing to listen to and accept new ideas and suggestions; open to new ideas and ways of doing things
recipient	a person who receives something
relationship-oriented	someone for whom relations at work are very important
reluctant	unwilling
report	someone below you in the organisation who reports to you
reprimand	expression of strong official disapproval to someone
resolution	an official decision made at a meeting, a conference, etc.
respondent	someone who replies to something like a questionnaire or a survey
(in) retrospect	looking back on a past event or situation

s

sceptical	doubtful about the truth of a claim or statement
self-esteem	how you feel about yourself. People with low self-esteem have a negative view of themselves. People with high self-esteem have a positive view of themselves
self-preservation	the act of being interested in your own situation and survival
sensitivity	an ability to understand what other people need, and to be helpful and kind to them

sidetrack	take a speaker away from the main point of the discussion, for example by introducing another subject
similarity	when two more things are quite like each other but not the same
sponsor	support a person, project, organisation or activity by giving money or other help
stakeholder	anyone who has a direct or indirect interest in the success of a business
struggle	have problems or difficulties
suspicion	a feeling or thought that something is wrong even if you cannot prove it
sustainable	able to continue over a period of time
synchronise	work together so that things move forward at the same time
systemic	affecting the whole of a department, organisation, system, etc.

t

tangible	something real which can be shown, touched or experienced
task-oriented	someone for whom relations at work are much less important than getting the job done
telco	a telephone conference
time out	a short break from a meeting, negotiation or other business situation
tolerant	putting up with things that you may not like or agree with, without complaining
tone	a quality of voice expressing a particular emotion, attitude, etc.

u

uncultivated	without good manners or good taste or much education
unforeseen	something that you did not see was going to happen

v

vendor	someone who sells something

w

webcast	an internet broadcast of an event, either live or recorded